SIBLEY'S
Birding Basics

ALSO BY DAVID ALLEN SIBLEY

The Sibley Guide to Birds
The Sibley Guide to Bird Life and Behavior
(illustrator and co-editor)

SIBLEY'S
Birding Basics

Written and Illustrated by
DAVID ALLEN SIBLEY

 Alfred A. Knopf, New York, 2002

Library of Congress Cataloging-in-Publication Data

Sibley, David, date.
  [Birding basics]
  Sibley's birding basics / David Allen Sibley.— 1st ed.
    p. cm.
  ISBN 0-375-70966-5
  1. Bird watching. 2. Birds—Identification. I. Title: Birding basics.
II. Title.

QL677.5 .S53 2002
598'.07'234—dc21   2002020768

Printed and bound by Artes Graficas Toledo, S.A.U., Toledo, Spain.
First Edition

Contents

Introduction   3

1. Getting Started   5
2. Finding Birds   12
3. The Challenges of Bird Identification   21
4. Misidentification   39
5. Identifying Rare Birds   52
6. Taxonomy   54
7. Using Behavioral Clues   60
8. Voice   66
9. Understanding Feathers   76
10. Feather Arrangement and Color Patterns   99
11. Structure of Tail and Wings   106
12. Bare Parts   119
13. Molt   123
14. Feather Wear   139
15. Age Variation   143
16. Ethics and Conservation   148

Latin Names for Species Mentioned in the Text   150

SIBLEY'S
Birding Basics

Introduction

A rose by any other name may smell as sweet, but without a name it is simply a flower.
> —Jim Wright and Jerry Barrack,
> *In the Presence of Nature*

Bird-watching is literally about watching birds, but it can be practiced in countless different ways. It can be scientific or artistic, technical or not. It can be done in one's backyard or in far-flung wilderness areas. It can involve simply identifying different species; or studies of the birds' songs, behavior, feeding habits, migration, nesting, and so on; or it may involve observing the interaction between birds and their environment—plants, insects, weather, humans, and so on. What all of these various approaches have in common is that they all require naming the birds—they all begin with bird identification. It is the challenge and the process of identification that is the primary focus of this book.

Bird identification in the real world is far more than just matching a picture to a bird. The fact that the living bird is a shy and wary creature, with no particular interest in being seen, means that the challenge of matching the details of the bird's appearance to a picture is compounded by the challenge of seeing and interpreting the details in the first place.

Ideally, all identifications would be based on an objective analysis of facts, clear observations of the actual appearance of the bird. In the field, however, identification is rarely 100 percent certain. One constantly encounters birds that are seen briefly or poorly, and in order to make an identification, one must make some judgment, some subjective interpretation.

This book is about interpreting what you see and hear in order to make better judgments. Most birds *are* easily identified—the trick is to know how to gather and weigh the evidence. The experts of bird identification do not have heightened senses as much as a better understanding of what they are seeing and knowledge of what they should be seeing.

This is not a guide to the identification of any specific birds. It is designed to promote a general understanding of the challenges of identification, and an understanding of how our impressions of the birds are shaped by the environment and the birds' behavior. This understanding will allow you to identify the common species with greater speed and confidence, tackle some of the really difficult species, and enjoy a greater appreciation of the birds themselves.

Acknowledgments

Many thanks to all the people over the years whose inquisitive minds and dedication to the art and science of bird identification have helped me to learn the basics of birding. Especially—the late Harold Axtell; Tony Bledsoe; Jon Dunn; Pete Dunne; Keith Hansen; Steve Howell; Kenn Kaufman; Bob Maurer; Noble Proctor; Peter Pyle; Will Russell; my father, Fred Sibley; and my brother, Steven Sibley; Rich Stallcup; Clay and Pat Sutton; and many, many others.

Special thanks to Chris Elphick, Steve Howell, Will Russell, and Joan Walsh for reading all or part of the manuscript and helping to correct and clarify many details. Any errors or misjudgments that remain are mine alone. Extra special thanks to my wife, Joan, for helping in so many ways, and to Evan and Joel for keeping my work from becoming my life.

1. Getting Started

Learn to See Details

One of the biggest differences between the expert birder and the novice is that the expert has spent years training to see details. The beginner must literally learn how to see them.

The challenge of seeing and interpreting details in birds is complex, and all of the issues are intertwined. A patient and deliberate approach and an absence of distractions are prerequisites. Active study, asking questions while observing, is important. Anything that promotes detailed study—such as sketching or taking notes—is also very helpful.

It is easy for a beginner to be overwhelmed by details and by the challenge and excitement of just seeing a bird. Not having a clear idea of what to focus on can result in an observation that yields no useful information. Experience will cure this, but as a general rule it is best to focus on the bird's bill and face. The shape of the bill will help you to place the bird in a broad group of related species, while the bill and the face together are a distinctively marked part of almost every bird.

You must not only practice seeing details but also practice seeing details at a distance. The field marks birders use at a distance are different from the marks used at very close range. Be conscious of this and study the birds to see how distance changes perception.

Watching a bird after you have identified it can be a very useful exercise. Watch it fly, watch it move around, watch it forage. Watch a bird as it flies away, but challenge yourself to identify it again based on what you can see at a distance. It's very important to know what you *cannot* see on a distant bird. You'll often hear experienced birders say something like, "I didn't see the white patch but I don't think it would have been visible at that distance," or "I didn't see the white patch, and it really should have been visible." This expertise can only be acquired by experience and by consciously testing the limits of perception.

Watch for Patterns

A large part of identifying birds is knowing what to expect. Having an idea of what you *should* see and simply looking for confirmation is far simpler and more productive than looking at a bird with no preconceptions. Every aspect of the birds' lives and appearance follows a pattern, and expectations of what species should be present and what they should look like are the precursors to quick and accurate identifications.

Birds are found at predictable times and places, and this information can be a very powerful clue. For example: A meadowlark seen in California can be safely identified as a Western Meadowlark based on the fact that the Eastern Meadowlark simply doesn't occur there. You do not need to study plumage details or hear call notes to feel confident in its identification as a Western Meadowlark. On a more subtle level, if the Red-tailed Hawk is the most common large hawk in your area, you can start with the assumption that any large hawks seen are Red-taileds. Then, looking specifically for a reddish tail, white speckling on the scapulars, the correct overall size or proportions, or dozens of other characteristics might be enough for you to conclude within a fraction of a second that you are looking at a Red-tailed Hawk. There is no need to consider other possibilities unless something doesn't match up.

Seeing and remembering all the details of variation in birds' appearance, habits, and distribution is much easier when one understands the underlying patterns. By paying attention to patterns, one develops a sense of the expected range of variation and can then quickly recognize and study any bird that doesn't match the expectations.

One of the most basic patterns that the bird-watcher needs to understand is the groupings of related species. Everyone knows that ducks are ducks and hawks are hawks. The birder knows that, among ducks, the diving ducks and puddle ducks are different; and that among the diving ducks, the eiders, scoters, scaup, mergansers, and others are all different. Even within the mergansers the Common and Red-breasted Mergansers are similar, while the Hooded Merganser is distinctive. Learning the characteristics that group related species together helps an observer to distinguish a duck from a loon, an eider from a teal, or a Red-breasted Merganser from a Hooded Merganser.

Gain Experience

Again and again in this book I will stress the importance of experience. There is no substitute for it. The methods and clues I put forth will be meaningful only after you have had some personal experience with them. The book covers some of the larger concepts; refining the ideas and filling in the details is up to the individual.

It is only through experience that you will be able to develop the detailed mental image of each species that is necessary for rapid identification. You should seek out more experience whenever possible, making an effort to see each species in different seasons or habitats. Seeing a bird in a different plumage or setting will give you a better idea of the range of variation in the species. More importantly, through this type of experience you can learn the essential characteristics of the species, the things that do not change regardless of plumage, season, or habitat. This information is essential in order to refine your mental image, prioritize the field marks, and arrive at an accurate identification.

One shortcut to gaining experience is to go out in the field with experienced bird-watchers. From them you will quickly and easily learn the basic techniques of birding as well as the common species in your area. Many birds are never seen well and so are difficult to identify without experience. To the novice this is just frustrating, but if an experienced observer can name the bird it becomes an opportunity to study field marks and to learn some valuable things about that species.

Most nature centers, parks, refuges, Audubon chapters, and bird clubs organize periodic bird walks, and the people who run these are always willing and able to help a new birder.

Learn from Your Mistakes

Another important bit of advice is to view mistakes as an opportunity for learning. Ask yourself why the mistake occurred. Perhaps you were just being lazy, perhaps jumping to conclusions on limited data, or perhaps you were misled because the bird was unusual or doing something unexpected. Perhaps you are familiar with the bird in a different setting and didn't know that it could look or act a certain way. Mistakes occur because of the pressure to make an identification quickly, based on limited clues. Analyzing your mistakes and those of others can be very enlightening.

It can be difficult to accept the fact that a lot of birds have to be identified as "possible" or "probable." There is nothing to be gained by convincing yourself that you have seen a certain species. Talking yourself into something or denying your mistakes will only slow the learning process and cause problems in the long run.

Equipment

Bird-watching requires very little equipment. In fact it is possible to take up bird-watching with no equipment at all, but a pair of binoculars and a field guide are considered the minimum. I also strongly recommend a field notebook.

Optics: Binoculars, Telescopes, and Other Gadgets
Many beginning birders are frustrated when they struggle to see the field marks that a more experienced birder is pointing out. The problem may be not the beginners' eyesight or ability but their binoculars. If you find yourself in this situation, you might want to investigate the possibility of buying better binoculars, as these can make a huge difference in the quality of your bird-watching experience.

Buy the best pair you can afford, and be sure to try them out before you buy. Seek advice from other birders and/or from a specialized bird-watching shop. Price depends more on the quality than on the power, and an image seen through more expensive binoculars is almost always brighter, more colorful, and sharper than one seen through a less expensive pair. The more expensive binoculars also tend to be more durable. Different makes and models have slightly different specifications. You might find that you prefer one model over another if, for example, brightness or close-focus is more important to you than weight, or you may simply want the brightest, sharpest model available in a certain price range.

I strongly recommend 7- or 8-power binoculars. The detail you see depends more on the resolution (sharpness) of the image than on the power. The advantages of these over the stronger 10-power binoculars is that they are usually lighter in weight; they present a brighter image; the inevitable vibrations from hand movement are less distracting; and the field of view is wider (you will see more of the habitat surrounding the bird). All of this makes it easier to locate, follow, and study a rapidly moving bird.

It's important to spend some time learning how to use your binoculars. Practice lifting them to your eyes and focusing on an object. Practice finding a specific leaf in a large tree by looking for landmarks with your naked eye and then following this "map" with the binoculars to locate the leaf. In time you will become proficient at locating even a flying bird in the binoculars.

For many types of birding—generally waterbirds such as sandpipers, ducks, and seabirds—a telescope is an essential tool. The telescope is useful not just for studying very distant birds but also for seeing fine detail on close birds. As with binoculars, you should buy the best telescope you can afford. I recommend a 30-power eyepiece with wide-angle view, if available. This is the highest power that can be used easily. Higher power magnifies the inevitable shake and wind movement, as well as atmospheric distortion, and is much more difficult to use to locate birds. You'll also need a sturdy tripod to mount the scope for viewing.

Many people pursue hobbies such as photography or sound recording along with birding. These can be useful to document what you are seeing for your personal enjoyment or to prove to others the sighting of a rare bird. The advent of digital cameras has made it very easy to take photographs or video directly through a telescope.

Field Guides

These are relatively compact books that describe and illustrate the key identification features for each species of bird. Most birders end up owning a variety of different field guides, and since each guide offers a different interpretation of the birds, it can be useful to consult more than one. At the same time, since using the guide requires a familiarity with the author's style of interpretation, you will probably develop a favorite guide, one that you feel comfortable relying on.

The field guide is a reference book as well as a learning tool. You should strive to learn the information included in it rather than use it as a constant reference. Too often, a birder barely looks at a bird before opening the book. By studying a bird, taking notes, and checking the book later, rather than immediately flipping open the book, you will learn far more. Similarly, by studying a bird even after the identity has been established, you can learn a great deal about that species.

You should mark up the book as much as you want. Write the date and location of sightings to help remember each species. Use a highlighter or add colored stickers to draw attention to the species that are most frequently seen in your area and help familiarize yourself with both the book and those birds.

Even though field guides include range maps showing which species might occur in your area, you can obtain much more detailed information from a local checklist or regional guide. Study this and mark in your field guide the species you'll be most likely to see.

Finding More Information

Allow birding to take you in other directions. Browsing technical journals can provide insights and bits of information that will help you to understand the birds and their identification. The more you learn about a bird and its habits, the better you will be at identifying that species the next time you see it.

Further Reading
As a bird-watcher, you should include at least one field guide in your library, and most of us find that over time we accumulate many books about birds. The second book in your library should be a guide to the status and distribution of birds in your local area; such books exist now for virtually every part of North America.

Allow your curiosity about birds to take you in other directions. There are literally hundreds of books about birds and every aspect of bird life. Remember that every bit of information you learn about a bird and its habits will help you to understand and identify that species in the field. Technical journals for ornithologists, such as *The Auk, Condor,* and *Wilson Bulletin,* provide fascinating reading for the motivated birder. Less technical journals catering to birders include *Birding* (the journal of the American Birding Association), *Birder's Journal,* and *Western Birds,* among others.

Comprehensive references such as the Birds of North America series, the Handbook of Birds of the World series, and Arthur C. Bent's Life Histories of North American Birds series provide detailed information about the natural history of the birds. For a more general overview of this topic try the *Sibley Guide to Bird Life and Behavior.*

For details about plumages, molt, subspecies, and other identification issues, the *Identification Guide to North American Birds,* by Peter Pyle, is an excellent reference. Many specialized books have been published recently on the identification and natural history of single families of birds, and more information is constantly being published. Yet even with all of this there are still questions that you will have to answer for yourself, and the path to increased knowledge involves both book study and field experience.

2. Finding Birds

One of the things that makes bird-watching exciting is that the birds are so mobile. You never know what you will see, whether you are going for a walk around the block or into a wilderness area. Similarly, the bird you see might be in view for only a few seconds before it flies off to some unknown place, and many species are simply elusive and secretive, reluctant to show themselves at all. To see birds you must be constantly alert, watching and listening all around.

Field Skills

• **Move quietly:** Birds are not necessarily disturbed by noises, but you may be distracted by them. Often the first clue to a bird's presence is some small rustling of leaves or soft call notes. Any noise or distraction, such as conversation or swishing clothing, can prevent you from noticing these signs.

• **Move gently:** Birds are extremely sensitive to abrupt movements. A sudden wave of the hand, such as that made when raising binoculars or pointing a finger, can scare off a bird more surely than almost any other action.

• **Travel slowly:** One can often see more birds by standing in one spot than by moving quickly and covering a lot of ground.

• **Watch for movement:** This requires holding still and looking with a "wide field"—not focusing on a particular spot. Once you detect a movement, even if you're not sure what caused it, you may find it useful to aim your binoculars at the spot and try to find a bird.

• **Follow sounds:** The expert finds many birds by knowing their songs and calls. You don't have to be able to identify the species to take advantage of one of the basic benefits of this. Simply listening to sounds will give you a clue to where the birds are in a given area, and then you will be able to walk toward them. This will maximize your chances of seeing birds, and you will see more of them than if you simply wandered around randomly. This is also a very important first step toward learning the vocalizations of the birds.

• **Pay attention to behavior:** Watch the edges of a flock and pay

Greater Yellowlegs looking up, perhaps at a hawk.

special attention to outlying birds or those that act differently; these may be different species. Behavior offers clues that can be a great help in finding and identifying birds, and noticing behavior is the way to learn these clues.

• **Let the birds find predators:** Birds' extraordinary alertness and eyesight can aid a birder. The scolding calls of chickadees, jays, or crows are often your first clue to the presence of a hawk or owl. Learn these sounds and track them down. Similarly, the alarm calls and evasive actions of small birds may also signal the presence of a hawk or owl. If all the birds at your feeder suddenly take off in a flurry of wingbeats and urgent high-pitched call notes, leaving the scene deserted and silent, you can be pretty sure that a hawk or other predator has just visited. A careful search of the ground or of nearby perches might reveal it, and the habit of looking out quickly when these sounds are heard will help you to see a hawk in the future. Take note when you see a shorebird cock its head to study something in the sky above. Look for whatever has caught the bird's attention and you may discover a high-flying raptor.

• **Watch flock behavior:** The takeoff of a flock of birds, or the coordinated movements of a flock of sandpipers in the air, takes on a certain urgency in the presence of a hawk. Many small birds react to an aerial predator by forming a tight flock and swerving back and forth around it, not allowing it to get above

Sharp-shinned Hawk with "ball" of European Starlings.

them or to single out one member of the flock. Starlings do this more dramatically and more persistently than other birds. The sight of a distant "starling ball" is often the first clue to the presence of a hawk.

Pishing

The making of hissing, shushing, and squeaking noises (known among birders as "pishing") is done in imitation of the scolding calls of certain small songbirds. It is often combined with imitations of the calls of a small owl in order to simulate the sound of an owl that has been discovered by songbirds. Birds approach to see what's going on and to join in scolding the predator.

Pishing is most effective when you are somewhat concealed within vegetation. The birds need to be able to get close to you without leaving their cover, and ideally there should be an open spot for them to sit when they do reach you. Curiosity will bring the birds in and then draw them to a perch where they can take a clear look at you.

Most birds will show interest only for a minute or two. Your best ally in pishing will be a curious scolding bird such as a chickadee or a wren. One of these species may show interest for minutes at a time, and its calls will bring in other birds more effectively than your imitations.

Pishing can be overdone; see my comments in the chapter "Ethics and Conservation."

Going Where the Birds Are

• **Consider the time of day:** One of the myths of bird-watching is that you must get up at the "crack of dawn" to see birds. While there is no doubt that the hour after sunrise is the peak of activity for many species of birds (and midafternoon is the low point), you can still find lots of birds at other times of the day. The activity of birds depends on the species and on factors such as temperature, weather conditions, season, tide, and what extra activities the birds are engaged in at the time (such as feeding young, migrating, molting).

• **Study edges:** Bird activity is often concentrated along edges—the edge of a lawn, pond, or woods tends to be more productive than the center—and you should search initially along these borders. On the other hand, don't just work the edges. Venturing into the heart of seemingly unproductive habitats can pay off with unusual or interesting observations.

• **Anticipate the birds' needs:** If you're looking for small land birds on a cold day, look along sunny edges. If it's windy, try to find a sheltered spot. If it's a hot day, look for cool shady spots with water. In dry conditions any small pool of water can be a magnet for birds. If you find one of these spots with a little bird activity, just sit down and watch; you'll get easy views of a steady procession of birds.

• **Consider the weather:** Experienced birders decide where and when to look for birds based largely on weather. A storm might require a check of local reservoirs or a coastal peninsula for migrating waterbirds blown in by the wind. A cold front in the fall or a warm front in the spring will bring a wave of migrating birds. By paying attention to weather patterns and bird movements you can develop much more detailed predictions of the "best" place to go birding each day.

• **Follow the birds:** If you find a number of birds in an area, consider why they might be there. Is there a concentration of food? Is it a warm or cool spot? If they're flying through the area, can you follow them to find a concentration point nearby, or back-track to find where they are coming from? Is it worth just stand-ing and waiting for more birds to come by? Whatever the reason, the same spot will be worth checking on another day.

Birding by Geography

Concentrations of migrating birds are often related to geo-graphic features. Some of the best-known places, and the rea-sons for their concentrations of birds, are described below.

• **Cape May, New Jersey:** Most birds are reluctant to fly over water, and the shape of southern New Jersey resembles a giant funnel, concentrating all southbound birds at the tip of the Cape May peninsula. The effect is most dramatic when a cold front and northwesterly winds push large numbers of migrating birds to the coast.

• **Monterey Peninsula, California:** Seabirds migrating south along the coast of California, and those foraging over the outer parts of Monterey Bay, are often pushed by prevailing westerly winds into the bay. As they move southward they encounter the Monterey Peninsula and swerve to go around it, concen-trating into a narrow band and passing very close to the tip of the peninsula.

• **Central Park, New York City:** Migrating birds that find them-selves anywhere in the vicinity of Manhattan gravitate toward Central Park, the largest patch of natural habitat in the area. The park acts as an oasis, the same way that a cluster of trees in the desert, or an island at sea, concentrates migrating birds.

These are dramatic examples of places that, because of geog-raphy, are among the best bird-watching sites in the world. By searching your local area for places with some of the same char-acteristics (even on a much smaller scale), you may be able to enjoy the benefits of birding by geography.

Attracting Birds to Your Yard

Of course, it is not essential to go out into the woods and marshes and stalk the birds. By providing food, water, and cover, you can bring many species of birds into your yard, where they can be studied at close range and watched at leisure.

Even if you live in a tenth-floor apartment, you can have bird feeders, and there is much pleasure and education to be gained simply by watching pigeons and sparrows at a feeder. A careful study of the plumage or behavior of one common species, or just a casual enjoyment of a variety of species, can be done from an easy chair in the comfort of one's own home.

Keeping Records

You are not required to keep any records while bird-watching, but doing so can speed the learning process, provide new incentives to go out, and increase your enjoyment of the hobby. There are many different ways to keep birding records, and your own method will develop with your specific interests.

The simplest and most popular form of record is simply a list of the species that you see in a particular time and place. Bird-watching and "listing" are almost synonymous, since one of the basic goals of bird-watching is to see new species, and keeping a list is simply a way to keep track of your progress.

The list that all birders keep is their "life list"—a tally of the species they have seen anywhere at any time. Many birders break lists down by regional subdivisions, recording birds seen in North America, or in individual states, counties, or parks. They also make lists for a year, a month, or even a special day, such as Christmas.

Although they may seem frivolous, these narrower lists have great benefits, as they encourage exploration. Much of our current knowledge of bird distribution comes from people who try to find a species in their home state or county or in a given day or year.

Field Notes

There are many methods of keeping field notes. You should choose the one that best suits you, depending on what it is that you want to record. Merely keeping a daily journal is the simplest, and it is very rewarding.

If you are recording dates, locations, and numbers of each species, a computer program is probably your best bet. Without having to make a prior decision about your specific interests, you can enter all your data once, and then you can generate reports that will show the species seen on a particular date, or in a particular location, or all records of any species.

There are now some excellent systems for handheld computers that allow you to enter data immediately in the field. But no matter what system you use, be sure you also have an easy method of recording brief notes or sketches about an interesting observation. Birds can never really be reduced to numbers in a spreadsheet, and you will always find a need to write some notes or do a little diagram or sketch.

Sketching

Sketching and taking notes are very valuable exercises that can increase your understanding and rate of learning simply by forcing you to translate what you are seeing into words and lines on paper. The act of doing that is enough to "cement" the memory, even if the sketch or words are a very poor representation.

Sketches used to record details of a whole bird: **Hammond's Flycatcher.**

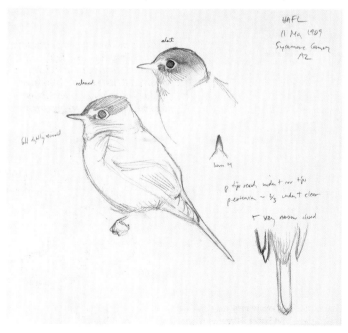

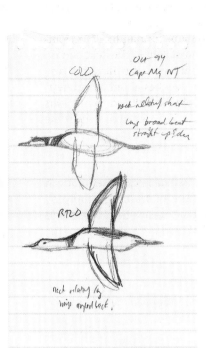

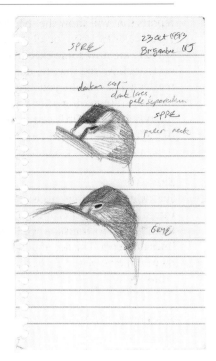

*Sketches made to show comparative details: **Common** and **Red-throated Loons** in flight (left); **Spotted Redshank** and **Greater Yellowlegs**, showing head shape and pattern when sleeping (right).*

*Sketch made to show very rough shape or wingbeats: **Winter Wren** in flight.*

A sketch demonstrates very clearly just how much you do *not* know about a bird. Don't be discouraged. By focusing on the weak parts of your sketch and trying to improve those aspects, you will advance more quickly.

Above are a few of my own field sketches, each made to record specific bits of information about a species. The combination of sketches and notes works well for that purpose. Although they look to some degree as if they were done quickly and casually, in reality each one is the summary of a long observation (in some cases hours) and careful study both before and during the sketching process. The vast majority of my time in the field is spent just watching and studying, and the sketches themselves take only a few minutes.

3. The Challenges of Bird Identification

You can observe a lot by just watching.

—Yogi Berra

Bird identification is like a matching game with a time limit. On one side you have images in a book or in your head, and on the other side you have a bunch of flitting, skulking real birds. Your challenge is to find those birds, see them well enough to discern a few characteristics, and use those clues to match the bird to the name.

The science of bird identification has evolved over the years, driven partly by advances in optics (allowing more detail to be seen) and partly by the gradual accumulation of knowledge about birds. The modern approach to bird identification centers on a holistic appraisal, studying the whole bird and considering everything from shape, movements, and color to molt, habitat, and date. In this approach, one might need to assess the wear of different feathers, judge subtle differences in bill shape or markings of particular feathers, or weigh the importance of a behavioral clue. The emphasis may be on looking at finer and finer detail, but the goal is to relate these minutiae to the larger picture of the overall appearance and behavior of the bird.

As your birding skills develop, your level of scrutiny will also change. The beginner might see just a flock of ducks. By identifying the species of ducks you will come to appreciate the fact that each one is not "just another duck." By looking still more closely, you will appreciate that individuals of each species, such as the Mallard, are not "just Mallards." Each individual can be scrutinized to determine its age and sex. Other clues may reveal evidence of hybrid ancestry or domestic strains, and then unusual variations of plumage or shape can be studied. You might notice behavioral differences between the sexes, or between individuals, and find that a world of information is opened up.

For the birder, one of the practical benefits of studying birds more closely is that the more precisely you define each species, the more accurate your identifications will be. The separation of the Least Sandpiper from the Semipalmated Sandpiper can be taken as an example. Making generalizations about plumage— "Least is browner than Semipalmated" or "Least has a darker breast than Semipalmated"—only allows you to identify some individuals and does not address variation in either species. Studying the color patterns of feathers to describe differences in more detail than "browner" or "darker" leads you to see much more concrete field marks and make more positive identifications. You'll need to understand statements like "juveniles have broader rufous edges on the tertials" or "adults' lower scapulars have anchor-shaped black centers," and this book will help you to do that. Remember that these are not just isolated details; they are related to other things such as the age of the bird or the position of the feathers and contribute to the bird's overall appearance.

Sorting Skills

Bird identification is all about comparisons. Whether you are looking at two birds side by side in the field or comparing a bird in the field to pictures in a book, you must make comparisons and search for differences. As I've said, you must train yourself to see details. Look at the two birds in the illustration opposite and make a list of all the differences you can see.

At first glance these are both bright red songbirds, but even a cursory study shows that they are different. Some obvious differences are the crest and the black face of the Northern Cardinal. Closer inspection reveals differences in the color and shape of the bills, the posture and proportions of the bodies, the shades of red, the shape of the wings, the length of the legs and tail, the color of the legs, the color of the edges of the wing feathers, the contrast between the back and breast color, the color of the flanks, and many other features. If we were in the field we would notice differences in behavior, food and habitat choice, voice, and so on. In fact one could go on in greater and greater detail listing dozens of differences between these two birds.

Now that you have compiled your list it should be clear that these two individuals are quite different. Let's add another bird. This gives you the sorting challenge of placing the birds in

Summer Tanager *(left) and* ***Northern Cardinal*** *(right): Can you find ten differences between these birds?*

groups based on the observed differences (see illustration below). Which ones belong together and which do not?

Sorting these birds into groups requires you to rank the differences, deciding which ones are important and which are not. Should the birds be sorted by color? By bill color? By head shape? By perching habits (on twigs or ground)? By some combination of characteristics? The immediate problem is deciding which of the observed differences are important.

At first glance the two red birds seem to be the obvious pair, but let's continue the exercise of looking for differences. Comparing the red tanager with the brown bird, we find that they differ in all of the ways described above, as well as in their overall color. Comparing the red cardinal with the brown bird, we find that these two differ in perching habits and in some details of plumage color. We may decide to ignore the differences in perching habits and overall color, knowing the inherent vari-

Two of these birds belong together. Which one does not belong? **Summer Tanager** *(left),* **Northern Cardinal** *male (middle) and female (right).*

ability of bird behavior and color, and to put more weight on the structural characteristics and color patterns. The best grouping of these birds, then, is to put the red cardinal and the brown bird (the female cardinal) together, despite the fact that the two red birds are so obviously and similarly red.

All of the many similarities between the two cardinals make it clear that these are very closely related—in this case, in fact, the same species. If we want to make generalizations to describe things that are common to all Northern Cardinals, we can describe a medium-size songbird with a rather long, rounded tail; short, rounded wings; a pointed crest; a heavy, red, conical bill; dark lores; and reddish wing and tail feathers. These are the fundamental characteristics of the Northern Cardinal. The fact that the male is bright red makes him stand out, but it is not an important part of the "essence" of the species.

There is a natural inclination to put a lot of emphasis on a bird's color, but again and again in bird identification, you will find that certain aspects of shape and structure are more meaningful than color. Features like bill shape and wing shape are very consistent within each species. The male and female, adult and juvenile, of nearly all species share a characteristic size, structure, and habits, and these contribute to the fundamental "look" of the species. All members of a species nearly always share some similar plumage and color details (such as the red-dish wings and tail, dark face, and red bill of all Northern Cardinals), and it is important to learn the fundamental details of plumage pattern that are common to all individuals of a species. One of the keys is to look past the brilliant colors and bold patterns of the most brightly marked birds, and to look instead for details of things like face and wing pattern.

The Northern Cardinal and Summer Tanager differ in dozens of details and can be identified by any combination of several of these details. The experienced observer can identify a cardinal just as confidently by the length and shape of the tail and the color of the undertail coverts as by the red crest and black face. You will learn to weigh different characteristics appropriately as you gain experience. Learning these associations, sorting the meaningful clues from the meaningless, and sorting the birds into groups can be very rewarding. You will experience great personal satisfaction in simply putting these clues together and knowing that you have figured out the name of a bird, similar to the moment of revelation and triumph when you suddenly know you have solved a key crossword puzzle clue or deduced the villain in a murder mystery.

Understanding Field Marks

Unfortunately, very few birds actually look like their pictures in field guides. The idealized portraits in a field guide show typical birds in perfect light, and usually no more than two or three of the most common variations of each species. In reality, every aspect of a bird's appearance is variable, and our impressions are further shaped by lighting and other circumstances of the observation.

There are many types of field marks, all with a wide range of reliability. Some field marks are very reliable and can work in almost any situation, while others can distinguish only some individual birds or work only under specific conditions. Understanding the value of different field marks, and how these field marks can work together to increase the accuracy of identification, is critical.

Many beginning birders hope to learn the "silver bullet"—the single absolute field mark that will distinguish all individuals of one species from any other species with total confidence. In reality, there are very few of these absolute field marks. Nearly every field mark, no matter how obvious or distinctive, can be absent or obscured, can be matched by variation or aberrant birds of other species, or can be misinterpreted by an observer. This is why no single field mark is ever enough to be the basis for an identification.

Another important point for beginners to understand is that bird identification is not an exact science and often does not involve absolute certainty. Nevertheless, in many cases you can be certain about an identification, and the more familiar or more distinctive species can usually be identified with certainty. The general goal, however, is to establish a level of "reasonable certainty" that is satisfactory. Different observers will set different levels, and some situations (such as the identification of rare species) will demand higher levels. The point is that you should not be afraid to consider field marks that are less than 100 percent reliable. Since no single field mark is ever enough to identify a bird, you must look for as many field marks as you can, and even vague and suggestive characteristics can be helpful. Use them wisely, along with other evidence, and they will become a very powerful tool for bird identification.

Relative Differences

Many field marks are relative differences; that is, they require some comparison, direct or not (for example, one species has a longer tail or a brighter yellow throat than another). Any comparative word such as "longer," "darker," or "coarser" indicates a relative difference. In field identification you must rely entirely on impressions and judgments, describing each species in reference to other species. Is a yellowlegs short-billed or long-billed? If you are most familiar with plovers you would say long; if you are most familiar with godwits you would say short. If you've been studying sparrows in dry brown weeds, an Orange-crowned Warbler among them will appear bright yellow. The same Orange-crowned Warbler among spring leaves with other warblers such as the Yellow and Blue-winged will look relatively drab olive-yellow.

Even when two species are together for direct side-by-side

comparison, one still needs to watch carefully and judge the extent of any relative differences between them. The Greater Yellowlegs is larger and longer-billed than the Lesser, but without reference points such as a side-by-side comparison, the differences can be very hard to judge. It takes a lot of experience to get a feeling for just how much bigger a Greater is than a Lesser before you can identify one with confidence.

The few nonrelative characteristics in birds are features like the red head of the Red-headed Woodpecker (it has a red head, other woodpeckers do not) or the wing pattern of the Willet (it has a broad white wingstripe, other shorebirds do not). It is true that other woodpeckers do have some red on the head (the Red-headed simply has more) and other shorebirds do have white wingstripes (the Willet simply has a bigger one), but these are fairly easy-to-judge field marks that even an inexperienced birder can use.

Proportional Differences

So far we've talked about relative differences by simply comparing one part of a bird to the same part of another bird. In the field we see the whole bird, however, and there is another type of relative differences that we can call proportional differences. For example, compared to the proportions of the rest of the bird and particularly to the size of the head, the Greater Yellowlegs's bill is proportionally longer than the Lesser's. Put another way, if the Greater Yellowlegs was shrunk down to the same overall size as a Lesser Yellowlegs, its bill would still look longer than the Lesser's.

In the example shown below, the Prairie Warbler appears longer-tailed than the Blackpoll Warbler, and most experienced birders would describe it that way. In fact, actual measurements show that the Prairie Warbler has a slightly shorter tail than the Blackpoll Warbler. The apparent length of the tail is affected by the overall size of the body, the length of the wings, and the length of the tail coverts. The smaller body, shorter wings, and shorter tail coverts of the Prairie Warbler make the tail appear longer in proportion to those other parts. In this case the impression (which is what really counts) is that the Prairie Warbler has a longer tail, and the field observer can say with confi-

Blackpoll Warbler *(left) and* **Prairie Warbler** *(right), showing differences in the apparent tail length.*

dence that the Prairie Warbler is proportionally longer-tailed, regardless of the actual measurements.

Average Differences

Average differences (which could also be called percentage differences or tendencies) are those that are apparent on some individuals but not all (for example, one species *tends to be* larger or brighter or more boldly marked than another). Western and Semipalmated Sandpipers illustrate a true average difference. Each species displays a range of bill lengths, but the average Western Sandpiper is longer-billed than the average Semipalmated. Despite the average difference it is quite possible to find a long-billed Semipalmated alongside a slightly shorter-billed Western. Given the slight overlap in the two species, and the difficulty of judging details of size in the field, many birds cannot be identified by bill length alone. The ones that can be identified by bill length are the extremes, the shortest-billed Semipalmateds and the longest-billed Westerns. The intermediate birds, on the other hand, must be identified by other characteristics.

There are absolute differences between most species, things that can be objectively measured so that 100 percent of the birds can be distinguished with no overlap. This may be true of birds in the hand, but in the field, because we must make subjective judgments, these same differences are less than absolute. The Greater Yellowlegs is always larger and longer-billed than

Western (upper two) and Semipalmated (lower two) Sandpipers, showing range of bill lengths.

the Lesser, and in the hand all of them can be distinguished by measurements alone, with no overlap. In the field, however, it often appears that the two yellowlegs species do overlap in size; that is, some yellowlegs appear intermediate, and size becomes, in effect, an average difference. Inexperienced birders may find size of little use in distinguishing the two species. As experience grows, so does the reliability of the judgment, but it never quite reaches 100 percent, and even the most experienced observers are occasionally confused by the size of a yellowlegs.

There is also variation in the degree of overlap in characteristics. Some average differences are easy to judge and can be used to distinguish 99 percent of the birds. Some are difficult to judge and almost entirely unreliable. The rest are somewhere in between. With experience you will get a sense of the value of each of these marks and your own confidence level and be able to weigh the mark accordingly. The more reliable differences carry more weight in the identification process.

While the weaker characteristics are only vague and subjective impressions that are almost useless for identification on their own, they are always interesting to watch for. They may contribute to an overall impression: for example, the bill of the Western Sandpiper also averages thinner and droops more at the tip, even when it is not longer than the Semipalmated bill, and together these subtle differences can impart a distinctive impression. With further study, some of the weaker characteristics might emerge as more reliable, and they may help in difficult cases as the supporting evidence, the tiny hint, that tips the balance one way or the other.

Accepting average differences as field marks means that any aspect of the birds' lives—behavior, voice, season, habitat choice, or migration timing—can be considered a field mark, as long as it suggests some difference between two species. Thus a bird can be identified based on a very general assessment of its appearance, the date and location of the sighting, and its behavior, all of which can be seen and analyzed in a split second at a great distance.

Separating Similar Species: Hairy versus Downy Woodpeckers

Discussing the various distinguishing characteristics of Hairy and Downy Woodpeckers provides a good general overview of some of the ways field marks are used to compare and contrast two similar species, and how different field marks are related.

• **Bill length:** The Hairy Woodpecker has a longer bill than the Downy, and there is no overlap in bill length. But because the field observer must rely on subjective judgments, the best we can do is say that the Hairy Woodpecker looks relatively long-billed, and this judgment is less than 100 percent accurate in the field. An observer's judgment of bill length is aided by the fact that, compared to the size of the head, the Hairy's bill is proportionally even longer than the Downy's. This makes it easier to judge the difference in bill length, and therefore makes bill length the single most useful clue.

• **Overall size:** The Hairy Woodpecker is always larger than the Downy, but, as with bill length, field observations of size are less than 100 percent reliable. Subtle impressions of differences

*Hairy Woodpecker (left) and **Downy Woodpecker** (right), showing differences in field marks. Eastern subspecies are illustrated; the western subspecies of both are darker overall but still show the same differences relative to each other.*

in structure, strength, and climbing or foraging actions might aid the experienced observer in judging overall size.

• **Voice:** These species differ in voice. Compared to the Hairy Woodpecker, contact calls of the Downy are relatively weak and low-pitched, the rattle call is shorter and weaker and descends in pitch, and the drumming is slower and more frequently performed. Experience is required to hear and assess these differences, but with practice, one can distinguish nearly 100 percent of these species by voice.

• **Tail bars:** In most parts of their range the two woodpeckers can be distinguished by the clean white outer tail feathers of the Hairy, and the presence of dark bars on the outer tail feathers on the Downy. Downy Woodpeckers always have black bars on the outer tail feathers, while most Hairys do not. Only the subspecies of Hairy Woodpecker found in Newfoundland and the Pacific Northwest often have dark bars on the outer tail feathers and therefore overlap with the Downy. This is the easiest field mark to judge, even for beginners, though it can be hard to confirm. It is very reliable in most areas, less so where Hairys have dark tail marks.

• **Extent of black on face and breast:** The Hairy tends to have more black on the face and breast than the Downy. The appearance of these markings, especially the amount of black on the breast, is highly variable depending on the bird's posture. The more solid dark lines on the face of the Hairy leading to the base of the bill might also contribute to the impression of a longer bill, while the more broken facial lines of the Downy do not. This is a subtle tendency that is generally true within a local region but varies according to the subspecies. It can be used only when comparing birds from the same local area, and then only as a weak supporting clue.

• **Nasal bristles:** The tufts of bristlelike feathers that cover the nostrils of the two woodpeckers tend to be bushier in the Downy Woodpecker and flatter and less conspicuous in the Hairy. This characteristic is probably most important as a contributing factor to the overall short-billed and "cute" appearance of the Downy. The flatter nasal bristles of the Hairy Woodpecker tend to emphasize the length of the bill, while the more tufted bristles of the Downy tend to break the line of the bill and make it look shorter. This is another weak supporting clue that is not reliable on its own but might be useful along with other field marks.

• **Foraging habits:** The Hairy is almost exclusively seen on trunks and major limbs of large trees, in more mature forest, while the Downy is often seen foraging on smaller twigs, or even on reeds or dry weed stems, and in the western states is restricted to riparian woodlands, especially willow tracts. This tendency is variable, with much overlap, but is very reliable at one extreme: A woodpecker on a twig or a weed stem is virtually certain to be a Downy.

Gestalt

Loosely translated, the word *gestalt* means "the whole that is greater than the sum of its parts." In bird identification this concept is used to refer to a distinctive overall appearance that is generated by the interaction of all parts of the birds, including subtle and indistinct characteristics. With experience, a birder builds up a mental image of each species that incorporates all aspects of appearance and actions to create an impression of the overall character of that species. At this level our bird identification technique approaches the way we identify our human friends, by indescribable subtleties of facial features, body proportions, and behavior.

Many birders use the term "jizz," which is apparently derived from the military acronym G.I.S., for "General Impression and Shape." This is similar to gestalt in concept, and the two terms are often considered interchangeable. The use of both terms in birding has broadened to include any group of subtle structural or behavioral clues, such as wing posture or wingbeats, that allow the observer to make an identification. These same clues can be described in words, and a birder should make every effort to do so rather than saying simply, "it had the right jizz."

Gestalt really refers to something much more ephemeral, an

Silhouettes of **White-crowned** *(left row) and* **White-throated** *(right row)* **Sparrows,** *showing differences in posture and shape that contribute to a gestalt impression.*

impression that cannot easily be captured in words. One classic example in gestalt psychology is that of a stock ticker or running headline sign in which flashing lightbulbs in the right sequence give the appearance of words moving across the sign. The parts—lightbulbs, wires, electricity—all together create something (motion) that is more than simply a collection of those parts. The same principle applies to the appearance of birds in the field, where posture, movements, and color patterns combine to create an overall effect that cannot be described by simply listing the detailed characteristics of the parts.

The differences in posture and overall shape between White-throated and White-crowned Sparrows involve gestalt in the interaction of many subtle features. Even though some of the differences can be analyzed and described in technical detail, your brain is taking in a huge amount of information and compiling an overall picture of the subtleties of shape and proportions from all angles. Thus it is often necessary and helpful to say that a bird has, for example, a "lankier" appearance, or a more upright posture, or a longer neck. It is important to be aware that there are really dozens of differences that combine to create the gestalt impression. Some of these, such as fleeting quirks of shape or proportion that show up momentarily as a bird moves around, certain sequences of appearance, or specific

*Two pairs of similar species, showing differences in facial markings: on the left, **Warbling** (upper) and **Red-eyed** (lower) **Vireos;** on the right, **Mew** (upper) and **Ring-billed** (lower) **Gulls.***

motions, are impossible to describe in words but may still be useful to draw attention to a bird or to support an identification.

The subtleties of gestalt can also be involved in our perceptions of the complexities of facial markings in some similar species (illustrated opposite). In the same way that cartoonists suggest expression by the tilt of an eyebrow, the facial markings of different species of birds can suggest different emotions. Thus Warbling Vireo and Mew Gull have a naive and gentle (blank) expression compared to the Red-eyed Vireo and Ring-billed Gull, which have a bolder, fiercer expression. Some of the differences can be described in more detailed and objective terms, but this involves many subtle features from bill shape to eye color. Any description is often unsatisfactory, as much of the impression is created by minute differences in coloration or behavior or by the interaction of many views from different angles.

Weak Average Differences

Even though a gestalt impression is real and significant, it is generally too "fuzzy" to be the sole basis for an identification. It is useful for quick identifications of common species, or for locating candidates for rare species, but a positive identification must be based on a more objective study of characteristics. In very similar species, such as many gulls, or Black-capped and Carolina Chickadees (illustrated below), these subtle and subjective impressions play a much larger role in identification.

Black-capped (left) and Carolina (right) Chickadees, showing weak average differences between these species.

Lacking any single reliable field marks, we must identify these species based on combinations of weak average differences.

The Black-capped Chickadee has, on average, a relatively larger head, overall larger size, fluffier plumage, a relatively longer tail, whiter neck-sides that extend farther onto the back, a greener back, brighter flanks, and darker wing and tail feathers with whiter edges (a more contrasting pattern). None of these features is reliable on its own, but taken together they create the overall impression of the Black-capped Chickadee as a larger, fluffier, more colorful, and more contrasty bird. An observer familiar with either species should notice an individual of the other species as an obviously different bird, but pinning down the differences is more difficult. In fact, closer study often seems to dilute the impression of differences.

Suppose you see a potential Black-capped Chickadee in the Southeast, where the species is not normally found. How can you be sure? The wing pattern is probably the most reliable of the differences, and you should start with that. Looking at other features in addition can build a stronger case for the identification. Even if each feature taken separately is only 70 percent reliable, the probability of all of the more typically Black-capped features occurring together on an individual Carolina Chickadee is very low. The more weak field marks you can add into the evidence, the more reliable the identification.

The concept that a few weak suggestive characteristics, taken together, can lead to a near-certain identification is used intuitively by the expert birder. Take, for example, an observation of a small bird with a longish tail flying around a suburban neighborhood in a flock, settling briefly in the highest twigs of a tree above a house. There are dozens of species of small birds with longish tails, and a number of species that might fly around a suburban neighborhood in a flock, but the only species meeting both of those criteria is the House Finch. Add to that the observation of the birds landing briefly in the treetops—typical House Finch behavior—and you can be virtually certain about the identification. The fact that this is all done without using any field marks in the traditional sense may be baffling to the novice, but to the experienced birder this is just a question of comparing observations to known patterns and seeing what fits.

Even though most of the bird is obscured by reeds, an experienced birder can easily recognize this as a **Red-winged Blackbird.**

Partial Cues

Imagine that you are peering through a stand of reeds and can just make out some movement. Looking through your binoculars and seeing bits of black and a flash of red, you can identify a Red-winged Blackbird. This is a very simple example of the use of partial cues. Parts of the bird are physically obscured, and your brain must construct a whole image from the fragments that are visible.

In a more abstract way, the same principle applies to most of bird identification. Seeing a distant bird in flight, you may get only a general sense of overall color, shape and wing proportions, and speed and patterns of wingbeats. These fragmentary clues are enough for the expert to sort and match to a known species that shows all of the observed characteristics. The fragments fall into place and allow a compilation of the whole.

While the expert may seem to have a mystical ability to discern detail and make an identification when you can see only a blur, the secret, of course, is familiarity and practice. We all perform equivalent feats every day. We recognize our friends and relatives simply by the way they walk or the way they tilt their head. You may be able to name the particular make and model of a car at a great distance, even if most of it is hidden behind a

Three words partially obscured, showing how partial cues can be used and misused.

building. Even a glance at a partially obscured or very distant sign can allow you to recognize familiar product logos. Your brain has a tremendous power to filter out distractions and fill in details of familiar patterns, and patterns in birds are no exception.

That said, there is a danger in filling in details in this way. You can jump to conclusions and convince yourself that certain desired details were actually seen. In the illustration shown here, a word is partially obscured by green coloring. You should be able to see enough to compile the entire word and read it as "BIRD." The upper image can only be the word BIRD; there is enough detail to confirm the identification. The lower two images also look like BIRD, but a cautious observer might notice that there are other possible identifications. The information observed there is not sufficient to rule out the possibility of "EIRE" for the middle word and "FIELD" for the lower word. Similar mistakes can occur in bird-watching, and it is easy to see from this example how one can be led by expectations to making an incorrect identification.

Bird identification is as much art as science. It involves subjective impressions of details of the birds' appearance and habits. It involves assessment of the reliability of the field marks and the reliability of the observation. It involves judgment and deductive reasoning to arrive at a "best fit" conclusion. It requires a balancing act between following expectations, yet not allowing them to bias one's judgment of subtle characteristics. It is extremely challenging from the very first moment, and as you gain experience both the challenges, and the satisfaction of meeting those challenges, will grow.

4. Misidentification

The eye sees only what the mind is prepared to comprehend.
—Henri Bergson

There are two separate issues that account for most species misidentifications. One involves the observer and normal birds that are either misjudged or misinterpreted. The other involves birds that are truly abnormal, such as hybrids and albinos. The overwhelming majority of problems is caused by the former.

Since most identification is based on judgment and on an observer's subjective interpretation of details, any birds seen briefly or poorly, which thus provide few clues to their identity, are likely to cause problems. There is a very fine line between making a "good call" and leaping to unfounded conclusions. You must maintain a balance between allowing expectations to lead you quickly to the "best-fit" identification and trying to identify with total confidence by considering each bird objectively. In either approach, it is important to know which field marks are reliable, and how much emphasis you should put on each of the observed marks. This involves not only the reliability of the field mark itself, but also the reliability of the observation. For example, you must ask yourself both "Does that species always have a longer bill?" and "How sure am I that the bill is longer?"

The importance of using multiple field marks should be obvious. They provide the supporting evidence that can clinch an identification, even when some field marks are inconclusive or not seen well enough for you to be certain. Many misidentifications arise from observers putting too much emphasis on a single field mark. You should learn and use supporting field marks that you can look for to confirm the identification. You will be much more confident knowing that several observed characteristics match up for a particular species.

It is also very important to be sure that the characteristics you are using are independent. "Larger size with slower wingbeats" or "darker back with darker tail" are examples of pairs of characteristics that are probably related and really don't count as multiple field marks. A bird that is larger is also likely to have slower wingbeats, whether it is a different species or not, or it may appear larger simply because it has slower wingbeats. A bird that is darker in one part could simply be darker overall, and therefore the darker tail means nothing. An observation of unrelated marks such as "larger size and darker tail" does count as two different field marks and provides much better evidence for an identification.

Unfortunately it is easy to bias your own observations through a sloppy or casual approach. By assuming that a bird is one species, and casually checking off features that support that identification, you can easily misidentify it. The first Calliope Hummingbird known to have occurred in New Jersey was identified by all who saw it in the field (myself included) as either a Rufous or Allen's hummingbird (two species that are virtually impossible to distinguish in the field). (It was correctly identified later from photographs.) Some questioned the identification at the time, and in retrospect the bird showed clear Calliope field marks. The experts, however, had the initial impression that it was "not right for Calliope" and therefore it was "about right for Rufous," and all of the contrary evidence was dismissed. This mistake was based in part on the expectation that a Rufous was more likely than a Calliope to appear in the Northeast in fall. Moreover, this bird, in a New Jersey backyard in November, did not have the same "look" as a Calliope Hummingbird in Arizona in August (where the experts had developed their expertise). Many out-of-place birds are overlooked simply because the identification process begins with the assumption that the bird could only be one of the usual species.

The same thing happens routinely in more mundane situations, more frequently than anyone knows. Beginners often find rare birds and assume that they are simply variations of the common species. Even more often they misidentify birds by starting with an incorrect assumption of size, occurrence, or other details. An observer studying a small sandpiper might conclude, based on the obviously long and drooping bill, that it is a Western Sandpiper, only to be told that it is actually the larger and longer-billed Dunlin. This mistake is based on the incorrect initial assumption that the bird is a Western, Semipalmated, or Least Sandpiper, ignoring the possibility of a Dunlin.

The converse happens just as often. An observer might see something intriguing, say a large falcon flying away, and jump to the excited conclusion that it could be a Gyrfalcon, a bird normally found in the far north. The next step should be to pause and start from the beginning, looking at each characteristic objectively, but too often the overexcited birder tends to stick with the first impression and simply tries to confirm the identification as a rare species. Often, a very brief sighting does not allow any more detailed study, and the observer might choose to emphasize anything that can tip the balance toward the desired identification: "Yes, it did look long-tailed; yes, it was very dark; it just didn't 'feel' like a Peregrine," and so on. Other poorly seen field marks that point toward a Peregrine Falcon—perhaps it looked pointed-winged, or seemed to have a contrasting white cheek—are then ignored.

This problem can result in a sort of "group hysteria" when large numbers of birders look at the same bird. The suggestion by one person that the bird is a certain species forms an expectation for everyone else, who then looks only for field marks to confirm the "expected" identification. In one very well documented case in California, the first state record of the Sky Lark (a Eurasian species) was misidentified for days, and by hundreds of people, as the state's first Smith's Longspur. These two species have a superficial similarity but are not even in the same family and can be distinguished by dozens of features. The initial observers expected a Smith's Longspur to show up in the state and never considered the Sky Lark as a possibility. Most of the people who went to see this bird over the next few days had the same expectation, augmented by the knowledge that they were looking for a "confirmed" Smith's Longspur.

Expectations, like all other field marks, are relative and average differences. They are one of the most useful and powerful clues to quick identification, and therefore one of the most important tools for the birder, but they cannot be relied upon. Looking at a bird with prejudice, having already determined that it is likely to be one species and seeking only to confirm that identification, will lead you into error. You should use expectations cautiously and take each step independently and objectively. Guard against forming an opinion until all of the evidence is in.

Judging Size

Size is often judged incorrectly, and this leads to many misidentifications. Birds reach their normal adult size within weeks after hatching and do not grow larger after that time. This fact and the relatively small variation in adult birds make size a valuable identification clue. Unfortunately the difficulty of judging size in the field makes it a frequently misinterpreted clue.

Use great care when judging size. Isolated birds may be impossible to judge correctly. Birds under unfamiliar conditions may appear very different from birds under more "normal" conditions. Accurately judging size requires extended careful study and comparison at multiple angles and views.

Consider the vague nature of the term "size." It could refer to total length, apparent body bulk, weight, and, for birds in flight, wing length and width. Try to avoid saying that a bird looks "bigger" than another. Instead use more specific words such as bulkier, longer-necked, broader-winged, and larger-headed. Each of these features can make a bird appear bigger, and each gives a much more accurate description than overall size.

Color can also influence the perceived size and shape of an object. Any bird seen against a strongly contrasting background color will appear larger than a bird that doesn't stand out from the background. In the example opposite, a typical Sandwich Tern with a mostly black bill is compared to a "Cayenne" Sandwich Tern (a subspecies found in the Caribbean and South America) with a yellow bill. Against an identical neutral gray background the yellow bill appears slightly larger and heavier. The implications of this, for identification that depends on careful assessment of bill size and shape (for birds such as gulls and terns, among others), are obvious.

Beware of judging size in comparisons with only one or a few other birds. These may not be typical and could give a skewed impression. Also be aware that apparent size is influenced by all kinds of environmental factors. Changes in feather arrangement in response to temperature and other factors can change the apparent size of a bird. Birds seen close to the horizon with trees or other objects in the foreground are interpreted by our

Sandwich Tern, *showing how color of bill affects apparent size: typical individual (left), "Cayenne" tern (right).*

brain as farther away and therefore appear larger than birds seen overhead with no reference points (this is the same illusion that makes the moon seem larger when it is close to the horizon). Fog or haze also makes a bird seem farther away and therefore larger. At twilight flying birds appear to have quicker wingbeats and smaller overall size than in daylight. Any physical condition such as molt that changes a bird's flight style can change the impression of size.

"Size illusion" refers to an optical illusion whereby objects that are farther away appear larger than closer objects of the same size when viewed through high magnification. This can have serious implications for anyone studying birds through a telescope or in photographs and trying to judge subtle differences in size. Awareness and an extra measure of caution are called for when you judge the size of birds through binoculars or telescopes.

Weather can also influence the apparent size of birds, as they fluff or sleek their plumage in response to temperature. Wind, too, can have a significant effect on their appearance. Perched birds tend to crouch down and face into the wind. Flying birds may adopt a different shape and flight style in wind. A bird flying into a head wind (or just trying to fly very fast in calm conditions) will sleek its body plumage and pull its wings in closer to the body to present a more streamlined shape. Wingbeats may be more forceful, deeper, and with more "wrist" action than under calm conditions. When flying into a head wind birds also tend to fly close to the ground (where wind speeds are lower), and any changes in flight path can be very abrupt as the wind "bounces" the bird around. All of these changes, from body and wing shape to flight style, can make a bird appear very different. Judging the size of distant flying birds relies

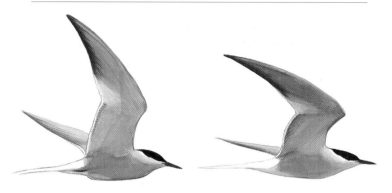

Common Tern, *in relaxed flight in calm conditions (left) and purposeful flight in windy conditions (right), showing how flight conditions can affect apparent size.*

partly on the quickness of movements and how much the bird seems to be "bounced around" by the wind. Clearly, these factors can be judged only under direct comparison with other birds facing the same wind conditions.

Judging Proportions

By definition, proportions are relative. One looks at bill size relative to head size, wing width relative to body size, and so on. Obviously a change in the size of one part affects the relative size of the other. Dramatic changes, from a fluffed, rounded appearance to a sleek, flattened appearance, can be achieved in seconds through muscular control of the feathers. Accurate judgment of proportions requires extended study at multiple angles. Under some circumstances a bird may not show a full range of postures even if you study it for hours. For example, in cold weather a bird will persistently keep its entire head and body fluffed up against the cold, which tends to make its bill look smaller than in warm weather, when all the feathers are sleeked down. The Herring Gull shown here demonstrates how the fluffed head gives the illusion of a smaller bill, and the sleeked head a larger bill.

A simple method of "measuring" part of a bird in the field is to compare it to another part of the bird. For example, rather than simply trying to judge the bill length of a Greater or Lesser

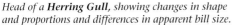

*Head of a **Herring Gull**, showing changes in shape and proportions and differences in apparent bill size.*

Yellowlegs, you can judge whether the length of the bill from base to tip is greater than the length of the head from bill base to the back of the head. If the bill length is much greater than the head length, the bird is a Greater Yellowlegs. On Downy and Hairy Woodpeckers and other short-billed species, the distance from the base of the bill to the eye provides an objective scale against which to measure the bill length. This will work in differentiating any proportionally different species. This method can also be used to take advantage of disproportionate differences between species. For example, the Glaucous Gull is relatively longer-billed but shorter-winged than the Iceland Gull. By comparing the bill length to the extension of the wingtips beyond the tail tip it may be possible for you to achieve nearly 100 percent separation of these two species.

Beware of the effects of foreshortening when you are viewing a bird. Seemingly simple tasks like judging tail length can be confounded by different angles of view. The simple solution is to watch a bird through many different positions to get a clear idea of the actual proportions. In certain situations, for instance at a feeder where birds are seen at only one angle or in the open where all birds are facing persistently into the wind, it may be difficult to get a complete range of views. You must guard against drawing conclusions from a bird seen incompletely under such circumstances.

Color Perception

Color is perceived relative to the colors around it. In the example shown below the same gull with identical gray back color is seen against a very dark and a very light background. The gray

Western Gull against different backgrounds, showing how the mantle color is influenced by the background color.

of the back appears darker when seen against a pale background and paler when seen against a dark background. This explains why gulls seen against snow and ice appear darker gray than at other times. Furthermore, the surrounding color influences the perceived color of the gray. Against a blue background the gray takes on a faint yellow-orange tone; against a yellow background it takes on a faint blue tone. This phenomenon may not often be evident in the field, but the basic point, that color perception is influenced by many factors, is worth remembering.

Light has profound effects on color perception. We automatically make allowances for much of this variation; for example, we expect a backlit bird to be a silhouette with little discernible color. Some of the effects of lighting are less obvious, yet they must always be considered when evaluating a sighting. As with other variable aspects of birds' appearance, you should try to watch a bird continuously through several lighting changes to get a complete sense of its color.

The Yellow-bellied Flycatcher shown opposite is seen in two extremes of light. The harsh direct sunlight in which you would encounter it at midday tends to wash out subtle colors such as yellow and olive, and the bird is dominated by contrasting shadows and highlights. The diffuse, even light that you might encounter on a slightly overcast day or in the early or late hours of the day reveals all of the bird's beautiful and subtle variations in color. The same bird can appear to be only faintly washed with yellow (left) or rich yellow-olive all over (right) and might be taken for two different individuals, or two different species, if the light is not taken into account.

Other effects of lighting include the suffusion of yellow or orange that occurs close to sunset, and the reflection of high-

***Yellow-bellied Flycatcher**, seen in bright sunlight (left) and diffuse soft light (right), showing how lighting affects color perception.*

lights on a bird's beak or plumage that can appear white or nearly white, even on a dark bird like a crow. Some species, such as shearwaters, have especially reflective plumage, and whole sections of their upperwing surface may momentarily glint with silvery-white reflections as they bank in flight. Many other species (perhaps all) show differences in perceived color depending on the angle of view, but the effects are generally subtle. In gulls, however, even subtle variations in the perceived gray of the mantle can be significant, and the angle of view does change the perceived tone of gray.

***Herring Gulls**, with bodies at different angles relative to the observer, showing slightly different shades of gray. A bird facing away usually appears darker.*

Color in birds' feathers can be created by pigments (red, yellow, black, and brown colors) or by structural features of the feather's surface, which may produce color by scattering (blue and bright green colors) or by iridescence (the bright colors of hummingbirds and the glossy sheen of species such as grackles). The pigment colors appear to be more or less similar regardless of the angle or type of lighting, while the other types of coloration are more strongly affected by differences in the light. The brilliant blue color of the Indigo Bunting or Blue Grosbeak can be essentially absent under dull light or backlighting. The gorget feathers (throat patch) of male hummingbirds are constructed so as to reflect pure color directly in front of the bird. One of these birds might appear to have a dull blackish gorget, perhaps with hints of yellow-green at certain angles, until it turns to face the observer and shows a flash of intense color.

Reflected light is another confusing factor. Some of the light reflecting off the bird has already reflected off another nearby surface, which transfers the color or brightness of that surface to the bird. Therefore birds flying over snow on a sunny day are brilliantly lit from below, as if spotlighted. Songbirds in dense foliage often take on a greenish glow from the surrounding leaves. Terns flying over green or blue water (particularly tropical blue water) show a reflection of that color on their white underparts. The underside of a male hummingbird's bill can reflect the red or violet color of the gorget feathers.

The most frequent lighting challenge facing birders is backlighting. Many birds are seen in poor light and must be identified based on features of size and shape along with whatever

White-winged Scoters, *as seen at a distance against a bright background, showing how backlighting "burns out" white coloration.*

plumage patterns can be seen. In some cases the pattern of translucent feathers on the wings can provide clues. You should always be aware under these circumstances that backlighting can alter impressions of size and shape. A silhouette against a contrasting bright background will appear larger than in a more neutral setting. Also beware that strong backlighting can "burn out" the light-colored edges of a silhouette, making parts of the bird appear thinner than normal. In the White-winged Scoters shown opposite, white wing patches essentially disappear, so that at a distance these birds can be identified by their "thin-winged" appearance.

Abnormal Birds

Occasionally you will find birds that you cannot fit into the standard categories. These are rare and in most cases are quite obvious, causing only momentary confusion, but sometimes they inspire long-lasting debates among birders.

The possibilities of variation in all aspects of a bird's appearance can result in individuals that are simply intermediate between similar species or that show conflicting characteristics. Some of these can be identified through careful study, others cannot. Still, it is always true that such birds are a tiny minority and should only be considered after other alternatives fail to explain the appearance of a bird.

The first challenge is simply to notice the bird. Since most birds are identified by the birder checking off a few key field marks and then moving on, a bird such as a hybrid that fits some of the expected characteristics can be overlooked, even if it shows other glaringly inconsistent features. It's abnormal, it doesn't fit anyone's search image, and yet most birders will never notice it.

Abnormal Plumages

The most common abnormal plumages are albinism and dilute plumage. Both these terms refer to a reduction of pigment in the feathers that causes a bird to appear to be entirely white (albinism), normally colored with patches of white (partial albinism), or normally patterned with the overall color reduced to a pale grayish or fawn color (dilute plumage).

Sometimes specific pigments are missing. There are records of birds lacking all yellow pigment but with otherwise normal plumage, or birds lacking black or brown pigment on some or all of their feathers but otherwise normal. Alternatively, certain pigments can appear in unusually high amounts, resulting in a bird that is overall blackish (this is known as melanism—an excess of melanin), or dark reddish brown, or other colors depending on the pigments involved.

Aberrations of pigment have many causes and appear in birds' plumages as a wide variety of conditions. The average birder, however, is unlikely to encounter any abnormally plumaged bird except for the partial albino (white patches) or one with dilute plumage (pale fawn-colored overall).

Occasionally birds become stained with oil or other chemicals, usually on the head or underparts, and these stains can give the appearance of abnormal plumage.

In all cases when a bird with abnormal plumage color is suspected, one cannot use color as a field mark. The identification should be based on clues such as the size, structure, habits, and voice of the bird, and to a lesser extent, the plumage pattern.

Bill Deformities

Rarely, birds with injuries or other conditions grow an abnormally shaped bill. The bill of all birds is actually a keratin sheath constantly growing over the underlying bone structure, and is maintained at its proper length through wear. Any condition that affects the normal wear of the tip of the bill can allow the bill to grow unchecked, and the result can be a grotesquely misshapen bill, such as a long, decurved bill like a curlew's, even on birds like chickadees.

Abnormal Size

Abnormally large and small individuals (giants and runts) are rare and probably do not survive long in the wild. There are a few documented cases, but these are so uncommon (and still relatively close to normal variation) that birders need not be concerned with the possibility of seeing one.

Hybrids

Hybrids are much more common than generally believed. Many of them are overlooked by people who simply ignore obviously "wrong" characteristics. Others are overlooked because they are so similar to the parent species. Identifying hybrids is a complicated process and requires careful study of all aspects of the bird. Many hybrids are intermediate between the two parent species, but others show unexpected characteristics. Hybrids are also highly variable, and even individuals from the same nest can show very different features. For an interested and motivated observer, a hybrid bird provides an unmatched challenge. It forces one to study the presumed parent species in order to find differences and assess variation, and then to apply those differences to the bird to determine whether it is in fact a hybrid of those species. Even after careful study, however, most such individuals must be labeled as "probable" or "apparent" hybrids.

Escaped and Domestic Birds

Beginning birders are often confounded by the ducks and geese they see on their first trip to the local park. These birds simply don't match up to anything in the field guide! Captives and domestic variants of certain species (especially the Mallard) show a tremendous range of variation. Many differ so profoundly in plumage and structure from the wild form that it is difficult to imagine they are the same species. But these birds are normally confined to urban and suburban parks and shouldn't cause confusion once learned.

Other species, from virtually anywhere in the world, do appear in the wild occasionally. These birds escape from zoos and private collections, and many of them acclimate and apparently survive in the wild for some time. If you find a very strange-looking and puzzling bird it may be worth checking other field guides to see if it could in fact be a species from another continent. Don't automatically assume that such birds are escapees from captivity; many species from other parts of the world have wandered to North America on their own.

Spoonbill Sandpiper, *one of the rarest—and most desired—birds in North America, among* **Western Sandpipers.**

5. Identifying Rare Birds

If you think that you, of all people, have found a rare bird, ask yourself the following questions:
Is this identification correct?
Can you think of even one explanation that works as well or better to explain what you have seen?
Do the marks you have seen really unquestionably lead to the identification as a rare species?
Are you being ruthlessly honest with yourself, or could you be suffering from wishful thinking?
    —Paraphrased from the *Annals of Improbable Research*

Finding rare birds is one of the principal goals of the serious birder. Locating and naming a species that is not expected is a great challenge and a great thrill, but it requires experience with all the topics covered in this book.

Be prepared to spend long hours in the field, accumulating experience with all the possible species. Seeing many birds in their normal range as well as out of that range will enhance your chances of finding a rarity. Familiarity with past patterns of occurrence in your area is also very helpful.

You must take great care to check all possible field marks and think of all alternative possibilities. Make sure you are using reliable, and reliably seen, field marks. Assessing these requires experience, too.

Reporting a rare bird carries some responsibility: Other birders are likely to invest time and money coming to look for it, and your report may be significant enough to be published—it becomes a part of science. If you believe that you have found a rare bird, study it carefully; try to document it with photos, video, or tape recordings; and take careful notes on the bird and the circumstances of the sighting. Then, as soon as possible, alert other birders.

6. Taxonomy

The gradual knowledge of the forms and habits of the birds . . .
impressed me with the idea that each part of a family must pos-
sess a certain degree of affinity, distinguishable at sight in any
one of them.

—John James Audubon

While sorting out all of the variations in the birds, it is helpful to know that ornithologists have been studying the same questions for centuries. Taxonomy, the classification and naming of living things, is basically an attempt to discern evolutionary relationships based on the fundamental similarities and differences among species. A group of related species forms a genus (plural *genera*), a group of related genera forms a family, a group of related families forms an order, and a group of related orders forms a class.

Modern taxonomy relies heavily on DNA analysis, but taxonomists also place birds into categories based on similarities of appearance and behavior; in short, the same things that birders use to distinguish species in the field. Birders will benefit greatly from knowing these categories and knowing the characteristics that are used to group species into genera and genera into families.

The urge to "simplify" by grouping the species according to superficial similarities of habits or (worse) by color obscures the important and fundamental characteristics that link evolutionarily related groups. Everyone would agree that ducks, coots, loons, grebes, and cormorants share certain habits and features in common and are often misidentified by birders. Placing them in their respective families emphasizes the fact that they differ in shape, structure, plumage, nesting, roosting, and feeding behavior, voice, flight, and so on. The differences far outweigh the similarities, and knowing the taxonomic groupings can help you get past the superficial similarities to see these differences.

You will notice that most bird books and bird lists present the species in a similar sequence. This arrangement is determined by taxonomists and is an attempt to group closely related

Four species of wading birds: from left to right, **Great Blue Heron, Black-crowned Night-Heron, Least Bittern, Sandhill Crane.** *Few people would guess that the two herons and the bittern are closely related and placed in the same family, while the crane differs in many aspects of structure, voice, and behavior, and is placed in a different family.*

species together. More distantly related species are generally farther apart on the list. In reality the relationships of birds form a branching tree like any family tree, and summarizing that complexity into a linear list of species is very difficult; nevertheless, the list itself conveys a lot of information about the evolutionary relationships and shared characteristics of the birds. Taxonomy forms the most important framework for understanding the patterns of variation in birds.

Bird Names

Common names of the birds have developed through long usage. They are convenient labels but they carry no deeper meaning, and some are actually inappropriate. Some species are named for people (Audubon's Oriole). Some are named for geographic locations (California Quail, which is common in that state; and Connecticut Warbler, which is rarely seen in Connecticut). Some are named for habitats (Marsh Wren, which is found in marshes; and Palm Warbler, which is usually not found in palm trees). Some are named for their songs or calls

(Whip-poor-will, which says its name; and screech-owls, which do not screech). Some are named for a superficial similarity to other, unrelated, birds (waterthrushes, which are not thrushes; and nighthawks, which are not hawks). Since the names were developed a century or longer ago, when bird study involved a shotgun and examination of museum specimens, we have birds named Yellow-bellied Sapsucker, Ring-necked Duck, and Sharp-shinned Hawk. These names describe characteristics that might be evident if you are holding the bird in your hand but that are difficult or impossible to appreciate in the field. Furthermore, common names differ widely around the world, and even the English names of some species differ (for example, the Black-bellied Plover in the United States is the same bird as the Grey Plover in the United Kingdom).

The scientific names, although less accessible, are much more valuable for the birder, since they impart real information about relationships among species. The scientific names are governed by rules of nomenclature and are standardized world-wide so that they transcend language barriers. The first word of the scientific name (always capitalized) is the genus. The second word (lowercase) is the species name. For example, the scientific name of the Semipalmated Plover is *Charadrius semipalmatus*. It is in the genus *Charadrius* and is distinguished from others in that genus with the specific name *semipalmatus*. The genus name is often abbreviated, so you might see it written as "Semipalmated Plover, *C. semipalmatus.*" Other species in

Five species of plovers representing two genera. From left to right: **Semipalmated Plover,** Charadrius semipalmatus; **Piping Plover,** Charadrius melodus; **Killdeer,** Charadrius vociferus; **Black-bellied Plover,** Pluvialis squatarola; *and* **American Golden-Plover,** Pluvialis dominica. *These are two of the three genera in North America that make up the family* Charadriidae *(Plovers and Lapwings), which is one of nine families in North America in the order* Charadriiformes *(including Sandpipers, Gulls, and Auks).*

that genus include *Charadrius melodus,* the Piping Plover, and *Charadrius vociferus,* the Killdeer.

Knowing that these species are in the same genus allows you to infer that they have more in common with each other than they do with, say, the Black-bellied Plover or American Golden-Plover of the genus *Pluvialis.* The plovers of the genus *Pluvialis* are larger, heavier, longer-winged, and differently patterned, with different calls and habits. The common name gives no clue that the Killdeer is a plover that shares many similarities in appearance, structure, voice, and habits with the Semipalmated Plover and others in the genus *Charadrius.* The common names also give no clue that the Black-bellied Plover and American Golden-Plover are very similar to each other, and different from Semipalmated and Piping Plovers.

Pay attention to genus names when browsing a field guide. Once you learn the characteristics of a genus you can apply that knowledge to any species that belongs to it and make comparisons to other genera: "All *Charadrius* differ from all *Pluvialis* in these ways. . . ." Thinking of birds in terms of genera, rather than species, can free you from repeatedly memorizing the minutiae common to all species in the genus.

The Species Concept

The definition of a species is subject to constant debate and revision by ornithologists, resulting in changes in the official lists of bird species. Decisions on recognizing new species or lumping together existing species are made by a committee of the American Ornithologists' Union and published in the *AOU Check-list of North American Birds.*

For the purposes of birders, a species can be defined loosely as any group of individuals that share similarities in structure, appearance, habits, voice, and DNA, and that tend to breed with each other rather than with other similar groups. Note that some interbreeding does occur; it is enough that the birds *tend* to mate with members of their own species. Evolution and speciation are ongoing natural processes, and there are many examples of "borderline" cases that can be resolved only by a careful consideration of all evidence and a judgment call by the AOU Check-list committee. New evidence and shifting opinions lead to changes in classification. The Baltimore and Bullock's Orioles, for example, long considered two species, were lumped into one species, the "Northern" Oriole, from 1973 to 1995, and then resplit into two separate species.

There is a continuum from well-defined and undisputed species such as Red-breasted and White-breasted Nuthatches, which differ consistently in structure, plumage, voice, habits, and many other details and never interbreed, to borderline species such as Glaucous-winged and Western Gulls, which differ in a few subtle and overlapping characteristics and interbreed extensively.

Subspecies

If the definition of a species seems a little ambiguous, the definition of a subspecies is positively fuzzy. A subspecies is considered any diagnosable population that does not rise to the level of a species. These populations occupy a defined region—their geographic range can be described—and all birds within that range show the characteristics of the subspecies. Simple variations that occur in some percentage of a species, such as the dark morph of Red-tailed Hawks, are not considered subspecies. Subspecies may differ from each other in plumage, voice, structure, habits, and even DNA, but the differences are slight, inconsistent, or not recognized by the birds themselves, so that interbreeding occurs freely wherever the subspecies meet. The characteristics of different subspecies are often related to climatic conditions such as rainfall, humidity, or temperature, and variation is most pronounced in sedentary populations (which can become more isolated than migratory ones). Far more variation occurs in western North America, where climatic conditions differ tremendously over short distances, mountain ranges tend to isolate populations, and many populations are sedentary. In most cases subspecific variation is subtle, and in many it is clinal (changing gradually across a wide area).

The Song Sparrow varies continent-wide and is separated into 29 or more named subspecies, but these vary only in details of size and the color and intensity of plumage markings. Their plumage pattern and most details of structure, voice, and habits do not differ among the subspecies. Most importantly, all subspecies of Song Sparrows seem to recognize themselves as Song Sparrows and interbreed freely wherever they meet.

The identification of subspecies can be a rewarding and exciting challenge. It is always complicated, however, by the presence of a significant number of intermediate birds. Whether these are intergrades between two subspecies or just variations of one subspecies, the fact is they make positive identification of these subspecies extremely difficult. Most attempts to identify subspecies must carry qualifiers such as "probably" or "showing the characteristics of. . . ." The quandary of subspecies identification is summed up neatly by Steve N. G. Howell (although he was writing about two species—Thayer's and Iceland Gulls): "We can't learn how much they interbreed until we can distinguish them, but we can't distinguish them because they appear to interbreed."

7. Using Behavioral Clues

The crow that mimics a cormorant is drowned.

—Japanese proverb

Learning the behaviors of birds can give you clues to identify birds, but more often it simply gives you the information you will need to better understand the differences in plumage and structure among species. A very subtle difference in wing shape might be related to a difference in flight style, which might be related to food choice or migration cycles. Birds are very efficiently adapted to their environment, and most of the characteristics of a bird can be related to some behavioral trait.

Always pay attention to the habits and to the placement of birds (you can expect to see the same species under the same conditions); watch for patterns; notice the vegetation—both the plant species and their structure. Soon you will notice much more subtle differences and develop a "feeling" about what you might see at each place or where to look for a certain species.

Regional differences in behavior are common. A specific set of conditions or type of food can cause the birds to engage in slightly different behavior. By studying birds in your own area you can observe tendencies that may be unique to the local conditions. These clues cannot be used as reliably in other areas, however. For example, experienced hawk-watchers develop a set of subtle, even subconscious, clues that they use to identify hawks at their home watching point. Traveling to an unfamiliar hawk-watching spot, these same observers can be totally bewildered by slightly different flight styles, different flight lines, and different angles of view or lighting.

Foraging

One of a bird's most important tasks is foraging. Much of the anatomical structure of the bird is related to finding and procuring food, and foraging behavior is intimately related to structure. Thus the different wing shapes of hawks and bill shapes of sandpipers, among many other examples, are linked to differences in food and foraging behavior, and because of these differences each species typically behaves in certain ways.

When you watch a bird feeder you will notice that each species uses certain foods and in certain ways. Chickadees choose sunflower seeds, flying in to grab a seed and then flying away. Goldfinches choose thistle seed, perching quietly and nibbling for minutes on end. Sparrows choose millet and hop around on the ground scratching or searching for food.

You can expect birds in natural settings to show similarly set preferences. Many behavioral traits allow you to place a bird quickly into a family or a group of species. For example, a small yellow bird that sits on a conspicuous twig for two minutes looking around is almost certainly a goldfinch and not a warbler. A small yellow bird that flits nervously through the vegetation, not sitting still for more than a few seconds at a time, is almost certainly a warbler and not a goldfinch. Woodcocks, snipes, and dowitchers, even though they are similar in shape and general habits, can always be distinguished by their habits and habitat choices. Robins flying onto a lawn swoop to a landing and hop two or three times before stopping; starlings fly down and land heavily, "sticking" to the ground.

More detailed observations reveal differences that can be useful in distinguishing species. Among the medium-size terns there are differences in the way each species normally dives into the water for fish. Black-chinned and Ruby-throated Hummingbirds (and other hummingbird species) hold and move their tails differently when hovering. Different species of dabbling ducks (genus *Anas*) tend to feed in characteristic ways. These differences are always tendencies, not reliable on their own to identify a species, but they can provide useful clues, even at tremendous distance.

Flight

Birds are often seen in flight, and you can learn to identify flying birds, but to do so you must know "the basics." Plumage patterns and bill shape can be seen in surprising detail on flying birds, as can leg length (useful on some sandpipers), and flight calls often provide the clinching detail. Size or bulk can be judged in flight, often more easily than on a perched bird. Quicker and more abrupt movements indicate a smaller and lighter bird, slower and more deliberate movements a larger and heavier bird; for example, you can often distinguish a Peregrine Falcon from a kestrel at a distance by the more direct flight of the larger Peregrine. Wing shape and body proportions (especially tail length) are very useful identification clues that can be more easily judged on a bird in flight than one on the ground. Don't be intimidated by flying birds; practice looking at them with binoculars and studying the details that you can see, and soon you will be sorting them out.

Many details of movement when the bird is flapping its wings and of the position of the wings when the bird is gliding provide useful identification clues. The rhythm of wingbeats, the arc of the wings during flapping (how high and low they reach), and wing position and action (swept back, stiff, snappy, and so on) can all be very helpful. Crows have a distinctive "rowing" wingbeat with most of the arc below the level of the body, and with the wings spread and pulled in with each flap; the birds flap almost continuously, and the flight path is nearly level, with no undulation. Other species with similar wing motions, such as the Blue Jay and Pileated, Red-headed, and Lewis's Woodpeckers, are described as having "crowlike" wingbeats. Experienced hawk-watchers distinguish Cooper's and Sharp-shinned Hawks at a distance mainly by judging the stiffer wingbeats of Cooper's or the snappier, quicker wingbeats of the Sharp-shinned. Common and Roseate Terns can be distinguished instantly almost as far away as they can be seen by the faster, stiffer wingbeats of the Roseate.

Modes of Flight

General modes of flight can be used to identify broad groups of species:

• **Bursts of wingbeats** and short periods of near free fall with the wings folded against the body, the flight path more or less undulating, are seen in most passerines and woodpeckers. The degree of undulation varies between groups and species, and depends on how closely the wings are held against the body. Species such as crows, which never pull their wings all the way in and flap fairly steadily, do not undulate much, while finches and woodpeckers, which close their wings tightly against the body between flapping movements, follow an extremely undulating path.

• **Continuous wingbeats** with little or no gliding, the flight path not undulating, are seen in waterfowl, herons, and many shorebirds.

• **Occasional wingbeats** with much gliding or soaring on outstretched wings are seen in the aerial species, such as gulls, raptors, swallows, and shearwaters. Within this group there are many specializations for different flight styles. Experienced hawk-watchers can identify most of the hawks they see just by wingbeats and subtleties of flight. The shearwaters perform a distinctive arcing flight known as dynamic soaring, which is also sometimes used by jaegers, gulls, and terns, even falcons, in high winds.

Variations in Flight Style

Differences sometimes occur in flight style depending on whether a bird is on a short- or long-distance flight; the Spotted Sandpiper, for example, uses stiff "stuttering" wingbeats on low, short flights, and much deeper, stronger wingbeats on high, long flights. Other species engage in unusual courtship flights or in "escape" flights that are very different from their normal flight style.

Flocking Behavior

Flocking behavior is another useful identification clue. Only certain species form flocks at all, and there are some subtle differences in their flocking habits. One of the most conspicuous flocking behaviors is flying in V or line formation. Commonly associated with geese, this habit is practiced by a number of other large species as well, including cormorants, ibises, ducks, swans, and even gulls and the larger sandpipers. Among the passerines that form flocks, careful attention reveals differences in the form the flock takes in different species. Watch for differences in the overall shape of the flock in flight (oval, tall, or stretched out, ribbonlike) and in the density (a loose association or a tightly packed mass). Study the movement of birds within the flock: Is the formation fairly stable or do birds move all around the flock? Simply paying attention and watching for these kinds of clues will enhance your observations, and may reveal other useful clues as well.

Seasonal Changes in Behavior

Another element that keeps bird-watching constantly surprising and exciting is the changing seasonal patterns of distribution and behavior. Birds that are conspicuous and common one month can be scarce and elusive the next. Migratory species can be absent one day and common the next. Understanding the seasonal cycles of the birds' lives increases our appreciation of the challenges they face—and may give us clues to a bird's identity.

You can expect to see different things each week throughout the year. What you are seeing now may not happen again until this same date next year. Even ancient observers noticed these cycles. This can be one of the most satisfying aspects of bird study, because it heightens and confirms our own sense of the grand seasonal changes that happen all around us.

The life of a bird centers on two or three main annual activities: breeding (from courtship to raising young), molt, and in many species, migration. In general, these activities all require a large investment of time and energy, so they do not overlap to any large extent. The winter season is also a challenging time for many species, particularly those that spend it in cold climates, and surviving the winter has a powerful impact on behavior in these species.

If you learn what behavior to expect at each time of year you will have a basis for some expectations of where birds can be seen at a particular time and what they might be doing. Throughout the United States and Canada, for example, the identification of spotted thrushes of the genus *Catharus* is simplified from November through March by the fact that only the Hermit Thrush normally winters here; all other species are far to the south during those months. Feeding behaviors and habitats also change; for example, many species of songbirds switch from a diet of mainly insects in summer to seeds or berries in winter and choose correspondingly different habitats. To find a Palm Warbler in Maine in June you would look in a spruce bog; to find one there in October you would look in a weedy field or in coastal dunes. To see a Common Snipe in the fall or winter you would search the edges of muddy pools near standing grass and weeds; on the summer breeding grounds you can often find one perched on top of a fence post or spruce tree, giving its territorial call. As with other aspects of bird behavior, each of these things is done for a reason, and all seasonal behavior relates to other aspects of the birds' structure, plumage, foraging, and their other behaviors.

It is important to know that all of a bird's characteristics are related. The bill length, leg length, neck posture, and other features are all specific to a certain lifestyle. Birds move or behave in a certain way in part because of their physical attributes. Sandpiper species don't just have different bill lengths and leg lengths, they have different postures, different feeding motions, different habitat choices, and so on that correspond to their structure. Each clue of behavior or posture helps the experienced birder read the clues of structure or plumage, and knowing the interrelationships of form and function leads to a better understanding of the bird. The expert birder is one who knows the whole bird in its environment.

8. Voice

There is about a bird song something that distinguishes the species to the practiced ear and that yet, after years of study, remains intangible and indescribable.
—Aretas A. Saunders, *A Guide to Bird Songs*

Identification of songs and calls can be the most frustrating and difficult aspect of bird identification to master, but for those who do learn it, it provides the greatest boost to birding skills— as well as a great satisfaction. There are some simple hints and techniques that can help you to get started learning bird songs. Voice identification is complex enough and different enough from sight identification that it can be classified as a specialized skill, but virtually all of the preceding advice about identifying birds by sight can be applied to the identification of birds by sound. You must make a conscious effort to learn the songs and calls, be aware, study, and practice. But be assured: the rewards will be great.

Variation in voice follows certain patterns, and taxonomy is one of the best indicators of variation. Related species tend to have similar calls and songs and similar repertoires of vocalizations. Studying the genus and family designations of each species, and mentally grouping related species, will help you in sorting out the variations in songs and calls.

Learning to Hear Details

When listening to birds, just as with looking at them, you must train yourself to notice the details. Birds' ears are much more sensitive than ours to the temporal details of sounds; some studies suggest that birds discern as much as ten times more detail in sounds than we do. So a very brief call note may contain a lot of information for the bird that hears it. You can't hope to hear it all, but you can train yourself to hear finer detail than you do now.

It may take a couple of years just to get your ears and brain "tuned in" to hear the differences between species. You will continually improve your ability to discern these songs and calls through practice. Beginners often listen to the same sounds as the expert but hear no difference. It's not that the expert has better ears, just a more discerning sense, like a practiced wine taster. The key to learning the details of birds' vocalizations is repetition. Concentrate on trying to identify every sound you hear. Track down unfamiliar songs or calls and try to identify the bird and watch it vocalize. The combination of hearing and seeing a bird call can help you to remember the sound. Other ways to enhance your memory are by trying to describe or imitate the sounds, and by taking notes and "drawing" them. These activities, like sketching, force you to listen in more detail and force you to interpret the observation in a form that will be easy to record. Any of these methods will help deepen your observation.

The Structure of Bird Vocalizations

Bird vocalizations vary in several characteristics: tempo (and pattern), pitch, quality, and loudness. Understanding each of these variables, and learning how to discriminate and describe them for any given vocalization, is fundamental to learning bird songs and calls. Most call notes are single short sounds that do not change much from beginning to end. Still, they can be short or long; their pitch can be high or low and rising or falling; their quality can be clear, buzzy, liquid, or other variations; and they can be loud or soft. Songs are generally more complex, with many changes during the course of the song. Understanding how to break a song down into its component parts allows you to describe each of those parts and to achieve greater accuracy and precision.

A complete song is generally constructed of a set of phrases, each of which is constructed of a series of notes. For example, in the song of the Scarlet Tanager each phrase is composed of several connected notes on different pitches, and the phrases are separated from each other by a slight pause. A set of phrases delivered with relatively short pauses constitutes a song, and the song is separated from other songs by a long pause. Listening to each of these parts in detail is the best way to study differences in songs. Songs of other species may consist of just a few simple whistled notes, or a rapid trill of the same note repeated many times a second, or a continuous warble of many notes continuing for a few seconds, and multitudes of other variations. In each case one must listen for pauses that distinguish phrases, the notes within the phrases, and the tempo, pitch, quality, and loudness of those parts.

Listen for slow or rapid tempo, short or long pauses between phrases, and short or long notes within each phrase. Also listen for short or long songs, and for short or long intervals between complete songs. All of these things influence the impression of tempo. Pattern is determined by the overall series of notes in a song, often including changes in tempo, such as the three-part song of the Tennessee Warbler. Tempo and rhythm are two of the most useful clues for distinguishing similar species. A well-known example is the Northern Mockingbird versus the Brown Thrasher. The mockingbird tends to sing the same phrase in a series three or four times, then pause before switching to another phrase. The Brown Thrasher sings phrases in pairs, giving each phrase two times and continuing quickly to another phrase, which is also repeated, and so on. The more halting and regimented pattern of the mockingbird's song—AAAA, BBB, CCCC . . . —contrasts with the steadier flow of the thrasher's song—AA BB CC DD. . . .

Listen to the overall pitch and to changes in pitch, noting whether the song varies widely from high to low pitch or is more even, and whether the overall trend of pitch in the song is rising, falling, or some combination. For example the songs of the Swainson's Thrush and the Veery are very similar in tempo and in their "spiraling" pattern, liquid quality, and overall pitch, but the song of the Swainson's Thrush begins at a lower pitch and rises, while the song of the Veery begins at a higher pitch and descends. Individual phrases in a bird's song might have distinctive patterns of pitch variation, such as the emphatic ending of the Chestnut-sided Warbler's song, which ends with a sharp rising and falling *meet-you*. It is generally easier to isolate the beginning and ending phrases of a song, but any phrase can provide identification clues.

The "quality" of the song refers to the "character" of the sound and is difficult to describe but can be very distinctive. It tends to be consistent within related species, so that, for example, the songs of all thrushes have a liquid, fluting, "thrushlike" quality. Quality allows you to quickly recognize a sound as typical of a group of species. Relatively obvious differences in quality make the distinction of Black-capped Chickadee and Golden-winged Warbler songs a simple matter, even though the species share a similar pattern of a long high initial note followed by lower notes on one pitch. The chickadee sings in a pure whistle, while the warbler sings in a very rapid, insectlike buzz, and these two species can never be confused.

Loudness, or volume, is generally not very helpful in identification. There is too much variation within each species, and too much variation depending on distance. Some species, however, sing songs that change in loudness. Examples are the Blackpoll Warbler, which sings a series of short notes on one pitch, beginning and ending quietly but becoming loud in the middle, and the Yellow-rumped Warbler, which also sings a song that characteristically begins softly and increases in loudness. The Greater and Lesser Yellowlegs and Hairy and Downy Woodpeckers are other species that can be distinguished in part by the loudness of their calls. In these cases the larger species of each pair gives a louder call, but given the variation in field conditions, what comes across is not necessarily a higher decibel level but a "stronger" sound.

Describing Songs and Calls

Each of the variables in bird vocalizations can be described, but each requires a different set of descriptive words. Describing songs and calls with words can seem hopelessly frustrating, and the results inadequate and sometimes misleading. The human vocabulary cannot convey the complexity of bird songs, and the limited vocabulary that has developed for describing these sounds often recalls the banter at a wine tasting: hollow, sharp, burry, metallic. Nevertheless, words are often the best method we have of recording these sounds, and there is value in written descriptions.

The rhythm (or tempo) of a bird's vocalizations can be described simply as hurried or relaxed, rapid or slow, regular or irregular. Individual call notes might be short and abrupt (or clipped) or long and drawn out. A rapidly repeated series of similar notes constitutes a trill, while an even more rapid series of similar notes is called a buzz. The pitch of a bird is either high or low and is best compared to that of other species. It is also very important to note whether a vocalization is rising or falling. Pitch is suggested by different vowel sounds: *ee* is the highest pitch, followed by *eh* (*ih*), *ah, oo, oh*. When saying these sounds in order you will notice the gradual change in shape of mouth required. Sounds can then be written as *tooee* for upslurred (rising at the end) or *teeoo* for downslurred (falling at the end).

Quality is the "jizz" of sound identification. Difficult or impossible to describe in words, it is the single feature that allows the expert to instantly identify fragments of birds' calls. Terms such as trilled, hoarse, liquid, sharp, and metallic can provide a starting point for describing the quality of bird sounds, but experience is the key. Keep in mind that many of the terms, and our impressions of quality, are inextricably connected to pitch and tempo, the other features of the sounds.

"Drawing" Sounds

Researchers who study bird songs use a computer to produce visual representations called sonograms. These essentially graph the sound, with the vertical scale going up in pitch, and with time running horizontally. A similar method of shorthand for sketching the characteristics of songs was developed by Aretas Saunders in the 1920s. Representing songs in this way is not only a valuable tool for recording and remembering sounds, but also a valuable learning tool, as it forces you to listen more closely and to discern all the different aspects of pitch, tempo, quality, pattern, repetition, and more.

A simple whistled note like the song of the Black-capped Chickadee can be represented by a simple horizontal line followed by another line slightly lower: *feee bee-eee* (below). The

more complex song of the Carolina Chickadee can be represented by horizontal lines on different levels to show the characteristic pattern of high-low-high-low pitch *fee bee fee bay* (below). A few words of description then suffice to indicate that the song of both species is a clear whistle. The graph tells us

that each note is level in pitch and that each note is separate and not connected or run together with adjacent notes.

Showing songs of three species of *Zonotrichia* sparrows can be done easily: The White-throated Sparrow song (below) uses the

same simple horizontal lines to represent clear whistles on a single pitch, repeated in a rhythmic pattern conforming to the familiar mnemonic *Old Sam Peabody Peabody Peabody....* Notice that each of the three-part phrases is about as long as the single sustained whistles at the beginning, so the tempo of the song speeds up considerably.

The Golden-crowned Sparrow (below) sings a song of three or so clear whistled notes, but at least one of the notes slurs down

in pitch with a smooth pitch change. This is represented by a curved line dropping down to show a whistle sliding down in pitch: *deeeee deeeaar doooo.*

The subspecies *gambelli* of the White-crowned Sparrow sings a more complex song (below). It begins with one or two level

clear whistles similar to those of the White-throated, but these are followed by two short phrases with abrupt pitch changes, then a series of separate, level buzzy or trilled notes: *seeee odi odi zeeee zaaaa zoooo.* The level, clear whistle at the beginning is followed by two short complex phrases that sound like two connected notes, the second one higher than the first, so they are drawn as two short horizontal lines connected by a vertical line. The buzzy notes at the end of the song are represented by a zigzag line. Rough or fine buzzes can be differentiated by the roughness of the zigzags, and even slurred buzzy notes can be shown by having the zigzag line rising or falling.

The distinguishing characteristics in the songs of another group of confusing species are relatively easy to see and to explain when the songs are graphed. The warbled phrases of the American Robin, Black-headed and Rose-breasted Grosbeaks, and Scarlet and Western Tanagers are generally similar and notoriously difficult to distinguish. Beginners have a hard time understanding what the differences are, let alone hearing those differences.

The American Robin (below) sings rapid phrases, usually four or five together, each clearly separated from the others by

pauses that are about as long as the phrases themselves: *eetaloo, ooti, ooti, eetaloo.* It often repeats the same phrase, so that a song might consist of a pattern like ABBA. Another song follows after a relatively short pause, and this performance may go on for many minutes. Repetition is common, and sometimes the same phrase is repeated eight or ten times in succession. The phrases themselves have a liquid quality, particularly in some of the transitions from note to note, and may recall the characteristic liquid sounds of other thrushes.

Rose-breasted and Black-headed Grosbeaks (below) sing a series of simple phrases at a relaxed and steady pace. Compared

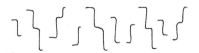

to the robin they sing more phrases, with shorter pauses between the phrases, so the song is longer and more continuous, and repetition of phrases is not obvious. After each song there is a long break before the next one. The phrases themselves are composed of softer notes than the robin's, with a husky or airy whistled quality rather than the robin's stronger fluting quality. Each phrase has a similar rhythm and a similar range of pitch, so that the song overall is a little monotonous, progressing methodically within the prescribed range.

Scarlet and Western Tanagers (below) sing a shorter series of phrases, run together with almost no pauses, so the song

sounds like a continuous burst. The phrases are varied—short or long, complex or simple, high or low—and thus the whole song is not as methodical as that of either the robin or the grosbeaks, and has a varied tempo and wide pitch range. Most distinctive for the beginner is the fact that the tanager species include some notes with a hoarse or burry quality, unlike either of the other examples.

Categories of Vocalizations

Each species has a repertoire of different vocalizations. The Yellow Warbler has a song (and distinguishable variations of the song used to communicate with other males or with females), contact call, flight call, alarm call, and other vocalizations less often heard. In comparing the voice of the Yellow Warbler with that of any other species you must compare only like vocalizations. The vast majority of vocalizations can be categorized as one of the basic types. Considering the context of each vocalization, as well as its sound, will help you to place it in the proper category.

• **Song:** This is the advertising vocalization for territory or mate, generally given by males during the breeding season and often accompanied by breeding displays. The courtship vocalizations of ducks, hawks, and some others are referred to as "display calls" or "courtship calls." They carry the same message as the songs of songbirds but are often not as complex or as aesthetically pleasing. The drumming of woodpeckers is also functionally the same as song. Many passerines have a primary and a secondary song as well as flight song or dawn song variations. A subdued version of song is sometimes heard, known as subsong or whisper song. In certain species such as vireos this whisper song is an entirely unique vocalization and not just a subdued version of the regular song.

• **Contact call:** All calls tend to be shorter, simpler vocalizations than song, and some are given by both sexes and at all seasons. The most frequently heard call note of most species is known as the contact call (for example, the sharp *chip* notes of warblers and sparrows).

• **Flight call:** Virtually all songbirds have a flight call, frequently heard and given either in the air or when the bird intends to fly (examples are the high *seep* or *zeet* notes of many warblers). This is the vocalization heard from nocturnal migrants overhead. The flight call is always unlike the contact call. Again, it is very important that you compare only analogous calls between species, that is, compare only flight calls with flight calls.

• **Other calls:** You may occasionally hear an alarm call, usually when you come close to a nest or young birds. In most songbirds this is a very emphatic version of the contact call, more or less so depending on the level of alarm. Threat calls (such as the harsh notes given by finches at a feeder during disputes) are rarely heard in the wild. Begging calls of young birds or courting females usually have a characteristic whining quality and differ between species. These can be useful for identification but are usually heard only for a few weeks each year. Other variations include close contact calls and courtship calls given by members of a pair at close quarters, and distress calls given by birds in trouble. Each group of species has its own particular categories of vocalizations, and certain variations may be given only by a few closely related species. For example, some *Empidonax* flycatchers have a "position note" given only by the male and mainly on the breeding grounds. This vocalization has no clear equivalent call in other species.

Variations in Calls

Contact calls and other call notes vary in volume, rate, and even quality and pitch depending on the motivation of the bird—an agitated bird gives louder and often sharper calls at a faster rate than a relaxed bird. Similarly, calls intermediate between different types may be given at times of intermediate activity; for example, a warbler giving a series of calls during takeoff might gradually change from contact call to flight call. In many species males and females give different calls (for example, the Red-winged Blackbird).

There is also variation among geographic regions, which may or may not follow the same patterns as the visual differences in the species. Most nonpasserine birds and a few passerines such as flycatchers inherit their vocalizations intact and do not learn them. Most other passerines partially learn their songs and some call notes, generally from their own parent and other local birds. These birds may develop dialects and other local variations; they may also incorporate the sounds of other species or unrelated environmental sounds into their own songs. Certain species habitually mimic the sounds of others: all members of the family Mimidae (to varying degrees), some vireos (such as the White-eyed), the Yellow-breasted Chat, goldfinches and the Pine Siskin, jays of the genus *Cyanocitta*, gnatcatchers, and the European Starling. Sometimes birds learn the "wrong" song. There are examples of a White-throated Sparrow mimicking a Black-throated Green Warbler, a House Wren mimicking a Carolina Wren, and many others. Voice, like any other field mark, should never be the sole basis for an identification.

9. Understanding Feathers

*Like Japanese haiku poetry, sometimes more is less; and in
nature, beauty or meaning need not be on a large scale.*
—Jim Brandenburg

Feathers are unique to birds and are virtually all we see of the
bird in the field. Understanding the arrangement of feathers
and how they relate to the bird's shape and color pattern is a
critical part of bird identification. Surely the feather is one of
the most remarkable structures in nature. Possessed by all birds
but by no other living thing on earth, feathers give birds their
brilliant colors and patterns, while also providing a lightweight,
streamlined coat that protects, insulates, and waterproofs.
Large feathers on the wings and tail make flight possible, while
spectacular ornamental feathers are used by some species in displays. Feathers are the feature allowing birds to exploit so many
diverse habitats and lifestyles, from deserts to arctic regions to
open oceans.

Scientists think that the original function of feathers was
insulation, to help the bird maintain a high metabolism and
high body temperature. Redpolls and other species weighing
less than half an ounce must maintain 105° F (38° C) body
temperatures while the arctic air around them dips to −30° F
(−34° C) or less! The importance of feathers to birds is demon-
strated by the fact that birds' feathers, as light as they are, commonly account for as much as 15 percent of a bird's total body
weight—about twice as much as its skeleton.

Numbers of feathers on an individual bird range from a minimum of 940 on a Ruby-throated Hummingbird to more than
25,000 on a Tundra Swan (70 percent of those on the head and
neck). Sparrows, such as the Song, White-throated, and Fox,
have 1,500 to 2,600 feathers—slightly more on larger species
and more in winter than summer. For the most part, larger
species of birds have larger feathers rather than simply more of
them.

This chapter will explore the details of feather structure, the
different types of feathers and their functions, and how all the
feathers on a bird's body work together to provide complete

*A **Purple Finch** with representative feathers from different parts of the body. On the left side is a range of feathers from the wings and tail; on the right side three body feathers. Note that feathers from different parts of the bird are specialized for different functions.*

and adaptable coverage—in short, how feathers define birds and how our image of birds is shaped almost entirely by their feathers.

Types of Feathers

Everyone is familiar with the basic form of a feather: a central shaft with a series of barbs on each side held together by tiny barbules to form a flat vane, or web. The length and stiffness of the shaft and the barbs determine the shape of the feather, while the number of barbules determines how tightly the web holds together. There are many variations on this theme, but all feathers share these same basic elements.

Almost all of the feathers we see in the field are classified by

Typical body contour feathers. Note that only the tip is brightly colored and that it is sturdier than the rest of the feather, with barbules holding the barbs together to form the vane, or web, while at the base of the feather the barbs are loose and downy. The web at the tip is the only part of the feather that is normally exposed.

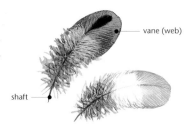

vane (web)

shaft

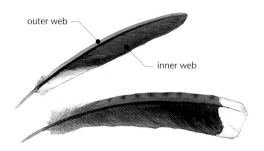

outer web

inner web

*Wing feathers of a **Blue Jay:** The outermost primary feather (upper) and one of the middle secondaries (lower), both from the right wing. Notice the asymmetrical shape of each feather, with the narrower outer web toward the leading edge of the wing.*

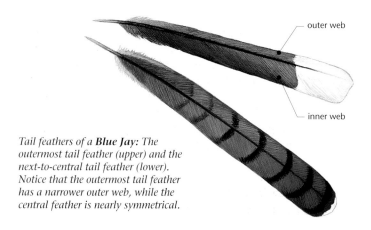

outer web

inner web

*Tail feathers of a **Blue Jay:** The outermost tail feather (upper) and the next-to-central tail feather (lower). Notice that the outermost tail feather has a narrower outer web, while the central feather is nearly symmetrical.*

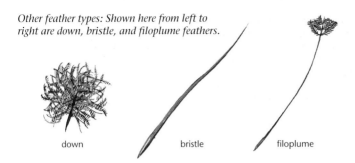

Other feather types: Shown here from left to right are down, bristle, and filoplume feathers.

down   bristle   filoplume

ornithologists as "contour feathers." We can subdivide these into two types: body feathers and flight feathers. Body feathers (the most familiar feather type) have a strongly curved shaft and are more or less symmetrical. These feathers create the outer "shell" covering the body and enclosing the insulating down feathers underneath.

Flight feathers are the long feathers of the wing and tail that function in flight. These have a very long shaft and relatively short barbs that are held together very tightly by barbules. Flight feathers are asymmetrical; the outer web is narrower than the inner web. Each feather is modified in length and shape for its particular function. Outer tail feathers, for example, have a shape different from inner tail feathers, and outer primaries differ from inner primaries.

Down feathers have a very short shaft and long flexible barbs with no barbules; therefore the feather is simply a swirl of soft barbs designed to trap air and provide insulation. The bristle is a specialized feather with almost no barbs, leaving only a stiff hairlike shaft. Bristles are found mainly around the nostrils, bill, and eyes, and function mainly to protect those parts. The filoplume is a specialized feather with a long slender shaft and a few weak barbs at the very tip. Filoplumes are found mainly around the neck and may function to give the birds information about the movement of other feathers. These specialized feathers are few in number, rarely visible in the field, and have little or no bearing on identification.

Cross section of feathers on body: Notice how the feathers grow up and back from the body, curving back and overlapping at the tips to form a smooth shell that traps a layer of air against the skin.

How Feathers Shape the Bird

Except in a few families (including penguins) feathers do not grow uniformly on a bird's body (the way hair uniformly covers a dog or cat). Instead, the feathers grow in tracts, leaving large areas of the body bare, and the feathers growing in the tracts must be shaped in such a way that they will cover the bare sections. The real marvel is that the resulting coat of feathers can flex, expand, and contract to provide full insulation and waterproofing even as the bird moves from swimming to flying to running.

Each feather grows out from the body and curves back toward the tail. In this arrangement each feather lies on top of the one growing behind it, only the tip of each feather is normally visible in the field, and all feathers overlap like shingles.

The actual body of any bird looks much like that of a plucked chicken; the feathers provide the familiar form. Each feather can be raised or lowered at will by the bird, using muscles at the

The visible outline of a bird changes with feather movements: bird with feathers puffed out (left) and sleeked down (right).

Laughing Gull, with feathers slightly raised or fluffed (left) so that each scapular feather is outlined distinctly, and with feathers sleeked down or compressed (right) so that individual feathers are almost indistinguishable.

base of the feather. The primary reason for raising the feathers is to trap a larger volume of air against the body for more insulation, as can be seen in the diagrams above. Notice that the outside appearance of the bird changes dramatically—from the sleek shape of an active bird in hot weather to the puffed-up shape of one in very cold weather—while the actual body size and the length of the bill and legs of course remain the same.

Given the possible changes in a bird's shape, you might think it would be difficult to judge its size, shape, and proportions. It is, but there are still strict limits to the changes that can occur— the feathers can move only in certain ways. You can use shape

Common Loon, showing how the shape of the head can change in several different ways, and how the shape of the neck and the resulting pattern are also variable.

Bridled Titmouse, showing crest raised and lowered.

and size as a powerful identification clue as long as you understand those limits.

The Concept of Feather Groups

Despite the variety of body types, habits, and colors of birds, there is remarkably little variation in the basic arrangement of feathers on birds' bodies. There are discrete groups of feathers on different parts of the body, each specialized for a particular function.

Ornithologists recognize seven major feather tracts on most birds, separated by unfeathered areas termed *apteria* (singular *apterium*). For birders it is useful to subdivide these tracts into smaller groups, each covering a specific part of the body. Feather groups can be distinguished by actual gaps, by underlying body contours, or by differences in the shape and arrangement of feathers. The result is a faint crease or seam evident

Song Sparrow, showing shadows along "seams" between feather groups. Any of these shadows can be reduced or enhanced by the bird's raising or lowering certain feathers, and should be borne in mind when you are assessing colors on a bird.

White-crowned Sparrow (any species of sparrow would be identical), showing organized arrangement of feathers, a grid with horizontal and vertical rows. Feathers on other parts of the bird are equally well organized.

where adjacent feather groups meet, and these seams can be observed in the field at close range.

Within each group the feathers grow in rows, in an organized pattern, and the length and shape of each feather is coordinated with those around it to provide complete coverage. This organization can be seen in any close study of a bird, and common patterns like streaking, barring, eye-rings, and wing-bars depend on such organization.

The feather groups are especially important for birders to know because they form the structural basis for the arrangement of feathers and color patterns on the bird. The basic groups can be distinguished on any bird, even an all-black species like a crow. Learning the groups enables one to describe any plumage markings accurately, and leads to an understanding of plumage patterns and of how those patterns can change as a bird changes body positions or moves its feathers.

Learning the groups and being able to interpret feather patterns at a distance requires plenty of experience. The good news is that you can gain experience by watching any bird. Pay attention to the feather groups and their variations on the gulls or ducks at a local pond, pigeons in the city park, or your pet parakeet.

Feather Groups of a Passerine

The diagrams shown here describe the basic feather groups for a passerine (songbird). The feather groups and their arrangement are remarkably uniform among the passerines, and one outline diagram of feather groups would work just as well for a crow as for a kinglet. Wood-warblers and sparrows have such similar feather arrangements that they all have the same number of rows of feathers on the breast and the back.

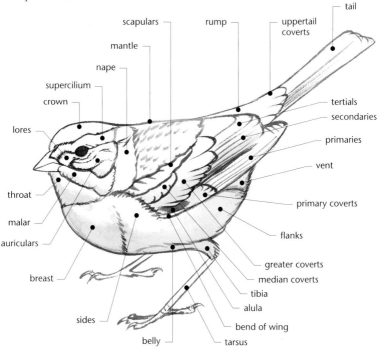

*The basic feather groups of a **Song Sparrow**, typical of all passerines.*

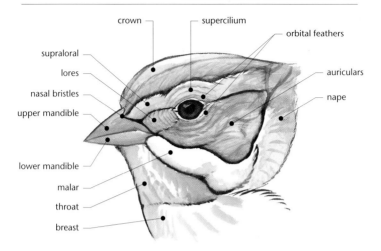

Song Sparrow, *showing details of head feather arrangement. Note how head feather tracts radiate from the base of the bill. Following back from the gape (the corner of the mouth) is a line that divides the auriculars from the malar. The malar is separated from the throat by a line running back from the lower corner of the bill.*

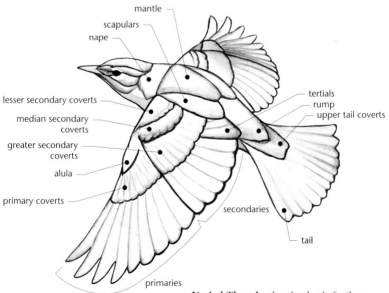

Varied Thrush, *showing basic feather groups of a songbird in flight.*

Feather Groups of Nonpasserines

There is more variation in feather groups among the nonpasserines than in the passerines, but in the diagrams that follow we can see how much all birds share in common. Compare the position of scapulars, wing coverts, auriculars, and other feather groups among the different bird groups. It is worth noting that waterbirds in any family tend to have a seamless feather covering on any part of the bird that is normally in contact with the water. Thus on ducks, gulls, sandpipers, and many others it is difficult to distinguish feather groups on the head or underparts.

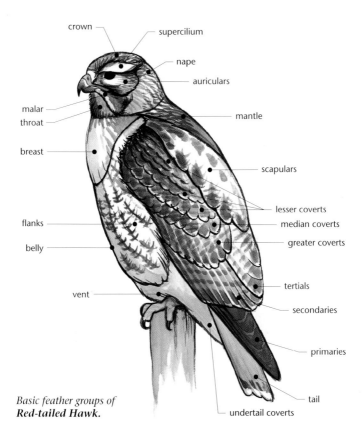

Basic feather groups of **Red-tailed Hawk.**

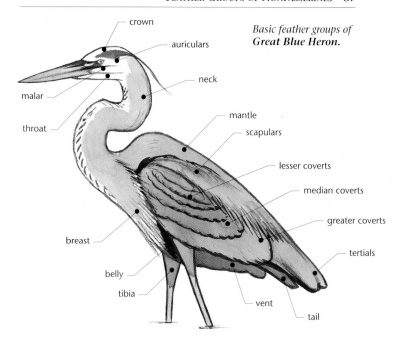

Basic feather groups of
Great Blue Heron.

crown
auriculars
neck
malar
throat
mantle
scapulars
lesser coverts
median coverts
greater coverts
tertials
breast
tail
belly
tibia
vent
tail

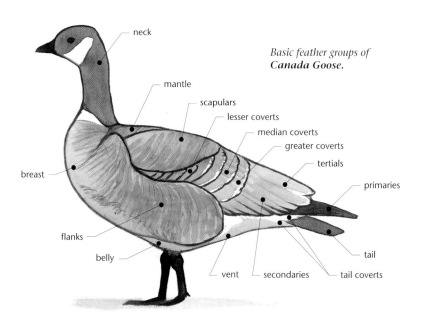

Basic feather groups of
Canada Goose.

neck
mantle
scapulars
lesser coverts
median coverts
greater coverts
tertials
breast
primaries
flanks
belly
vent
secondaries
tail coverts
tail

Basic feather groups of
Northern Pintail.

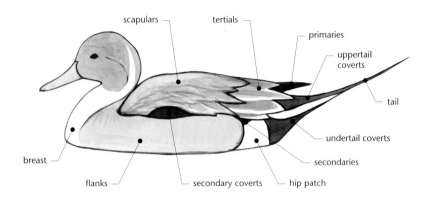

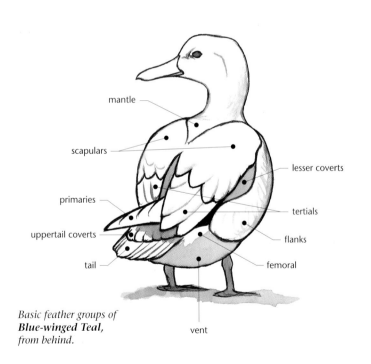

Basic feather groups of
Blue-winged Teal,
from behind.

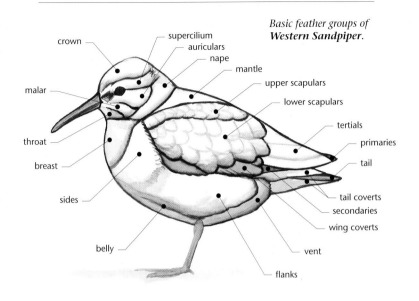

Basic feather groups of
Western Sandpiper.

crown
supercilium
auriculars
nape
mantle
upper scapulars
lower scapulars
malar
tertials
primaries
throat
tail
breast
tail coverts
secondaries
sides
wing coverts
belly
vent
flanks

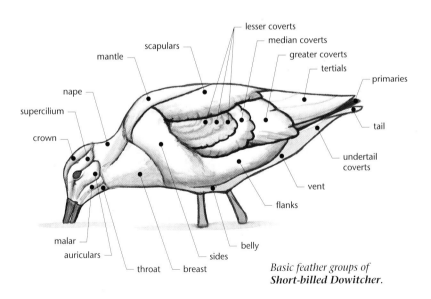

lesser coverts
median coverts
greater coverts
scapulars
tertials
mantle
primaries
nape
supercilium
crown
tail
undertail
coverts
vent
malar
flanks
auriculars
belly
sides
throat
breast

Basic feather groups of
Short-billed Dowitcher.

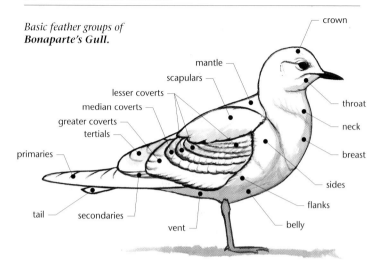

Basic feather groups of **Bonaparte's Gull.**

crown

mantle

scapulars

lesser coverts

median coverts

greater coverts

tertials

primaries

throat

neck

breast

sides

tail

secondaries

vent

flanks

belly

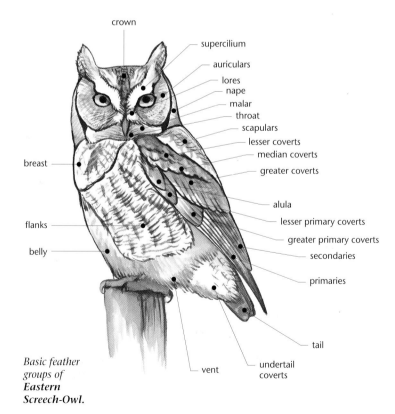

crown

supercilium

auriculars

lores

nape

malar

throat

scapulars

lesser coverts

median coverts

greater coverts

breast

alula

lesser primary coverts

greater primary coverts

flanks

secondaries

belly

primaries

tail

Basic feather groups of **Eastern Screech-Owl.**

vent

undertail coverts

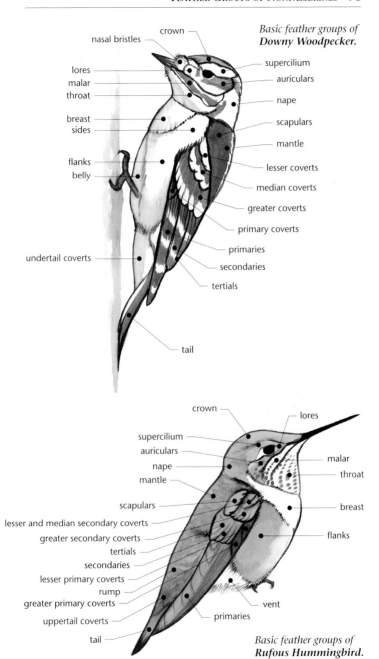

Basic feather groups of **Downy Woodpecker.**

crown
nasal bristles
supercilium
lores
malar
throat
auriculars
nape
scapulars
breast
sides
mantle
flanks
belly
lesser coverts
median coverts
greater coverts
primary coverts
primaries
undertail coverts
secondaries
tertials
tail

crown
lores
supercilium
auriculars
nape
malar
mantle
throat
scapulars
breast
lesser and median secondary coverts
greater secondary coverts
flanks
tertials
secondaries
lesser primary coverts
rump
greater primary coverts
vent
uppertail coverts
primaries
tail

Basic feather groups of **Rufous Hummingbird.**

Body Feathers

• **Nape:** The back of the neck; relatively long fluffy feathers wrapping around the sides of the neck behind the auriculars to the end of the malar. The area of the nape behind the auriculars may be referred to as the *neck-sides.*

• **Mantle:** The upper back; long like the nape feathers but sturdier and often boldly patterned; arranged in neat rows to form streaks. Broad pale outer edges on the symmetrical rows create pale *braces* on many species. Note that "mantle" is also commonly used to refer to the entire upper surface of the wings and back in gulls.

• **Scapulars:** Feathers inserted on the "shoulder"; these feathers spread to cover the base of the wing in flight. On passerines the scapulars are relatively inconspicuous, duller, and less distinctly patterned than the mantle feathers; they are much more prominent on nonpasserines and are often boldly patterned or ornamental. The degree to which scapulars are exposed and to which they cover the wing on a resting bird is variable. Gray scapular bases are obvious on birds that are puffed up because of cold or illness. The small pale *scapular crescent* at the base of the tertials of many gulls and terns is formed by white tips on the rearmost scapulars.

• **Rump:** The lower back. When the bird is perched, the rump feathers lie under the wings, while the mantle feathers lie above them. Thus the rump is nearly or entirely concealed by the tertials, and the scapulars appear to intervene between the mantle and the rump. Rump feathers are long and fluffy, weakly patterned relative to the mantle, and can be fluffed out to cover the wings during very cold weather. Most birds that are called "white-rumped" or "yellow-rumped" have only the lower part of the rump colored; in dowitchers the entire rump is white. The term "rump" is also used loosely to refer to any contrastingly colored patch in the vicinity. On birds like the White-rumped Sandpiper and Northern Harrier the white "rump" is actually white uppertail coverts.

• **Uppertail coverts:** A graduated group of stiff feathers overlapping the base of the tail to provide streamlining. The central feathers are long while the lateral feathers are short, creating a triangular grouping.

• **Breast:** A triangular patch below the throat; these feathers actually grow from the front of the neck. Breast feathers are often streaked, and the central breast spot that is such a common and variable feature of many species is partly a result of the convergence of feathers at the lower border of the breast.

• **Sides:** A poorly defined group of feathers intermediate between the breast and flanks that overlap the bend of the wing. There is often a spur of dark color extending down from the upper back along the line between the breast and sides, and patterns of streaks usually differ slightly between breast, sides, and flanks.

• **Flanks:** Long loose feathers along the sides of the body that can be fluffed out to cover the wings.

• **Belly:** The center of the underside of the body; this area is generally unfeathered, but several rows of lower flank feathers grow inward to cover the bare patch of skin. A seam is often visible along the midline of the belly, ending at the lower border of the breast and at the vent. Belly feathers are often unpatterned and/or whitish in contrast to flank and breast feathers.

• **Vent:** A transitional area involving several small groups of feathers between the flanks/belly and the undertail coverts, including on many species a patch of dense fluffy feathers between the legs, often whiter than the surrounding feathers.

• **Undertail coverts:** A graduated group of relatively long feathers overlapping the base of the tail below; these feathers move with the tail.

• **Femoral tract:** Just forward of the tail insertion, a patch of relatively small, tight-fitting feathers that are overlapped and mostly covered by the long rear flank feathers, but usually visible from the side just below the primaries. Especially well developed in waterfowl, sometimes appearing as a prominent light patch; can be called a *hip patch.*

• **Leg feathering:** Generally insignificant. Passerines have the tibia covered with short, usually drab, feathers. Some non-passerines have the tarsus feathered as well.

Wing Feathers

• **Primaries:** Long feathers growing from the "hand" bones and forming the lower border of the folded wing, numbering nine or ten on passerines, up to twelve on nonpasserines. The tip of the longest primary usually extends beyond the tip of the longest tertial. The length of this *primary projection* is often a useful field mark.

• **Secondaries:** Long feathers growing from the "forearm" bones, numbering nine to eleven on passerines and ranging from six on some hummingbirds to twenty-five on some vultures. On the folded wing only the outer edges of the secondaries are visible, and extensive pale edges then may create a *secondary panel.* Most dabbling ducks have an iridescent patch, commonly referred to as the *speculum,* on the upperside of the secondaries. Pale bases of the secondaries (often extending onto the primaries) form a *wingstripe.*

• **Tertials:** Three feathers, actually the innermost secondaries. The innermost tertial is short, and the outermost is usually longer than the secondaries. On the folded wing these broad feathers overlap most of the secondaries to protect them from the elements. Pale outer edges may create a bold *tertial stripe.* When the wing is folded, pale tips on these feathers form the *tertial crescent* seen on gulls and terns.

• **Greater coverts:** The largest of the coverts (small feathers that cover the bases of other feathers), generally one for each secondary and tertial. The inner (tertial) coverts differ in shape and color from the outer (secondary) coverts. Pale tips on the greater coverts form the *lower wing-bar.* Technically these greater coverts should be called the greater upper secondary coverts, but it is understood among birders that the unmodified "greater coverts" refers to these feathers and not to the greater primary coverts or the greater under secondary coverts.

• **Median coverts:** A row of relatively short, broad feathers overlapping the bases of the greater coverts. Pale tips on these feathers form the *upper wing-bar.*

• **Lesser coverts:** Small feathers overlapping the bases of the median coverts up to the leading edge of the wing. These are relatively inconspicuous on passerines and are usually concealed by the side feathers when the wing is folded, but are much more obvious on long-winged species such as gulls and sandpipers.

• **Marginal coverts:** Tiny feathers on the leading edge of the wing.

• **Primary coverts:** Narrow, stiff feathers overlapping the bases of the primaries; usually barely visible beneath the greater coverts.

• **Alula:** Three or four feathers on the "thumb"; usually just the outer (lower) edge is visible on the folded wing.

• **Axillaries:** A group of feathers radiating from the base of the wing and covering the underside of the base of the wing; prominent only on long-winged nonpasserines. Functionally the same as the scapulars, which cover the upperside of the base of the wing.

• **Humerals:** A group of feathers growing from the humerus of very long-winged species. Humeral coverts cover the base of the humerals. The inner humerals are broadly overlapped by the scapulars.

Head Feathers

• **Crown:** A continuous strip of feathers covering the top of the head from the base of the upper mandible to the back of the skull. The crown feathers are short (except in crested species) and rigidly arranged, with a fairly abrupt transition to relatively longer, looser nape feathers at the rear. *Forehead* is an imprecise term for the forward part of the crown reaching the bill; the forehead blends imperceptibly with the crown feathers to the rear. Many species have a pattern of darker feathers along the sides of the crown and paler feathers in the center, creating dark *lateral crown stripes* with a pale *median crown stripe.* Any more or less central patch of contrastingly colored feathers on the crown is called a *crown patch.*

• **Supercilium:** A strip of feathers beginning at the base of the upper mandible at the nostril and extending back along the side of the head above the eye to the back of the head. The supercilium feathers can be distinguished from the crown feathers by the fact that they grow out from the side of the head and curve upward, while the crown feathers grow up from the top of the head and curve back and slightly down. A slight "ridge" is often visible on the sides of the crown where the supercilium and crown feathers press against each other. This long strip of feathers can actually be separated into three distinct parts. Between the eye and the bill above the lores is the *supraloral* or *fore-supercilium,* made up of the first rows of normally shaped but very small feathers above the lores. The ***true supercilium*** is composed of several rows of small feathers above the eye extending back to just above the rear edge of the auriculars. The ***rear supercilium*** extends from the back of the auriculars around the back of the head but is really nothing more than the transitional area between the crown and the nape. Any part of this strip of feathers can be contrastingly colored. Differences in the shape of a pale "eyebrow" stripe along the supercilium (which can be a very important identification clue, for example, between the two waterthrushes) are the result of differences in color pattern, not in the shape of underlying feather groups. The pale eyebrow stripe does not necessarily follow the outline of the supercilium feather group.

• **Lores:** A patch of tiny bristly feathers between the eye and the bill, arranged in concentric arcs in front of the eye. The loral feathers merge imperceptibly with the auriculars below the eye and are usually weakly patterned and dull colored but can be quite striking (a good example is the Black-capped Vireo, in which the entire lores are white and along with the white orbital feathers form a unique variation of "spectacles").

• **Auriculars:** The cheeks or ear coverts, a complex set of feathers covering the side of the head below and behind the eye. Generally arranged in concentric rows below the eye, these feathers become larger to the rear and the rows flare. Where the auricular feathers actually lie over the ear opening they are lacy and open, allowing sound to pass through. These form a small area of weakly patterned grayish feathers on most songbirds, through which the ear opening itself may be visible as a small dark smudge. Feathers growing around the ear opening are short, very sturdy, and densely colored, designed to channel sound into the ear and forming a very well defined border of the auriculars. Small clusters of feathers in this area may be contrastingly colored, and the resulting patterns are complex and variable. The term ***post-auricular spot*** has been applied to any of these contrasting markings around the back of the auriculars, which need to be better defined for accurate descriptions of patterns. The ***eye-line*** or ***post-ocular line*** is formed by the uppermost auriculars, beginning at the rear point of the eye (where it actually intervenes between the upper and lower orbital feathers), ending and flaring at about the rear edge of the auriculars.

The *lower auriculars* are a more or less rectangular group of feathers growing at the lower edge of the auriculars, projecting into the malar and forming most of the lower border of the auricular complex. The *moustachial stripe* or *sub-auricular stripe* is a common marking on many species involving the lower edge of the auriculars from the lores to below the eye, often continuing along the lower auriculars; it is typically well defined against the malar but not well defined upward or rearward.

• **Malar:** The feather group covering the side of the lower jaw, beginning at the base of the mandible and extending back to the neck. This feather group is well defined at the front but merges at the rear with the throat and with the neck-sides. It is sometimes called the *sub-moustachial stripe.*

• **Throat:** The area spanning the underside of the lower jaw. This feather group is well defined on either side, separated from the malar by an unfeathered strip originating at the lowest point of the base of the mandible, but to the rear the throat blends imperceptibly with the breast feathers. The *lateral throat stripe* or *whisker line* is a common marking on many species; it is a dark line formed by the outer rows of the throat feathers bordering the malar. (It has been called the malar stripe, but this marking usually does not involve any malar feathers.) The *median throat stripe* is an uncommon marking (common in hawks and herons) involving a dark stripe down the center of the throat. The *chin* is the front (upper) end of the throat, the tiny point of small feathers right at the underside of the mandible, which are often contrastingly colored but difficult to see in the field.

• **Orbital feathers or eye-ring:** Several rows of tiny feathers encircling the eye and flaring at the rear. These rows are well defined above and below the eye, but merge with the loral feathers in front and do not enclose the rear. Patterned with great variation but remarkably consistent within any species, the coloring around the eye can be a very important identification clue. The inner rows of orbital feathers may be light-colored and along with the small fleck of intervening feathers at the rear may form a *complete eye-ring* (as on the Nashville Warbler). Pale inner rings along with small sections of outer rings can create distinctive lopsided eye-ring shapes (as in the

American Robin), while variations of **broken eye-rings** or **eye-arcs** are created by a few dark feathers interrupting the light ring (also in the American Robin). **Spectacles** are formed by an eye-ring connected to a pale supraloral stripe (the Blue-headed Vireo, for example).

• **Nasal bristles:** A small tuft of bristles covering the nostril. They are well developed in corvids, and the size or color of these bristles can be a useful identification clue in some closely related species (Chihuahuan and Common Ravens, for example).

• **Rictal bristles:** Relatively long "whiskers" growing around the base of the bill. These are thought to protect the eyes from stray bugs. They are virtually never useful in field identification but can provide some help in the hand (for example, the Common Yellowthroat is the only wood-warbler that lacks rictal bristles).

10. Feather Arrangement and Color Patterns

Feathers are the building blocks of all color patterns on birds. The patterns are created by the markings and shapes of individual feathers, and by the feathers' overall arrangement. Since the arrangement is predictable, and is consistent within large groups of species, there are limits to possible color patterns, and there are features that are shared in similar form by most species.

Many of the patterns are created simply by solid-colored feathers arranged in specific ways, usually along the contours of feather groups. For example, the dark breastband of the Semipalmated Plover is created by a band of solid black feathers surrounded by solid white feathers. In other patterns, such as the streaks on the mantle of the Song Sparrow, the individual feathers are patterned. A few common feather markings are seen repeatedly in many variations and combinations in all species of birds. The six basic types shown here create most of the patterns. When we examine the overall patterns in the context of the underlying feather groups, the basis of the patterns is usually deceptively simple.

Six basic feather patterns: from left to right, streaked, spotted, barred, vermiculated, edged, and notched.

Streaking

Streaked underparts are a common feature of many birds, from sandpipers to sparrows. Considering the orderly arrangement of feathers, one need only draw a dark line down the center of

*Three species of small songbirds, showing fundamental similarities in pattern: **Savannah Sparrow** (top), **Yellow Warbler** (lower left), and **Dark-eyed Junco** (lower right).*

each to create the typical streaked pattern. In the illustration above, the Savannah Sparrow and Yellow Warbler look very different overall because of their color. A careful examination, however, shows that the pattern of streaking, based on the arrangement of feathers, is essentially identical in these and all other small, streaked songbirds. The Dark-eyed Junco illustration shows how the edges of the feathers, aligned in rows, can create a faint suggestion of streaks even in a species without a streaked pattern, simply because of the way the feathers are arranged.

Overall Patterns

Given that the color patterns of birds are based on an orderly arrangement of feathers and a few basic feather patterns, it should be possible to deduce the pattern of individual feathers needed to to create an overall pattern. The illustration opposite shows a Short-billed Dowitcher with selected individual feathers. Studying the patterns of these feathers should give you a sense of how the overall pattern is created.

Short-billed Dowitcher, *with selected feathers to show how the patterns of individual feathers combine to create the overall color pattern.*

Head Patterns

The arrangement of feathers on the head is the most intricate of any part of the bird. This fact, combined with the strong signaling function of head patterns, leads to an incredible variety of markings, which are some of the most important and distinctive field marks in identifying birds. Despite the variety of patterns, there are many similarities in head patterns among different species. Just like patterns on other parts of the bird, the head pattern largely follows the arrangement of feather groups. Knowing these feather groups is fundamental to understanding the head patterns; at the same time, studying the details of head patterns can clarify the underlying feather groups.

The pattern of feather arrangement on the head is relatively complex. Rows of densely packed, tiny feathers radiate back from the base of the bill and encircle the eye. The feathers are smallest at the base of the bill, becoming gradually larger toward the back of the head. Specialized feathers cover and surround the ear opening. Different feather groups originate at different parts of the bill, and studying the base of the bill is the key to distinguishing the various feather groups. With experi-

Head patterns of four species of warblers: **Yellow Warbler** *(upper left),* **Blue-winged Warbler** *(lower left),* **Prairie Warbler** *(upper right), and* **Townsend's Warbler** *(lower right). Note that the pattern of dark markings on the head more or less follows the contours of the common feather groups, and that a subtle pattern can be detected even on the "unpatterned" Yellow Warbler.*

ence much of the intricate variation in head patterns becomes clear.

The concentric rings of tiny feathers around the eye are often entirely or partly colored so as to form an eye-ring. This may be broken by dark feathers front and rear as in the American Robin and Yellow-rumped Warbler, broken just in the front as in the Blue-headed Vireo, or unbroken as in the Nashville Warbler. On the Yellow-rumped ("Myrtle") Warbler the upper eye-arc is connected to a white area extending back along the supercilium. In all cases the differences in pattern are the result of tiny differences in color. The underlying feathers are identical in all of these species.

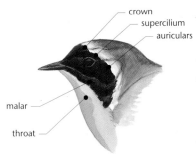

crown
supercilium
auriculars

malar

throat

Common Yellowthroat, *a species with a head pattern that does not follow feather groups. While the lower border of the black mask follows the line separating the malar and throat, the upper border of the black mask cuts across the crown, across the supercilium just above and behind the eye, then across the rear corner of the auriculars.*

Head patterns of four songbirds, showing how details of pattern are usually related to head feather arrangement. Upper row: **Yellow-rumped ("Myrtle") Warbler** *(left),* **American Robin** *(right); lower row:* **Nashville Warbler** *(left), and* **Blue-headed Vireo** *(right).*

The tiny feathers between the eye and the bill just above the lores, the supraloral, are also often contrastingly colored in whole or in part. When wholly colored (as in the Blue-headed Vireo) the result is "spectacles." When partly colored the result is a white supraloral spot, as on the Yellow-rumped ("Myrtle") Warbler and American Robin, or a faint supraloral streak, as on the Nashville Warbler.

The pattern on the malar of these species is worth studying as well. On the Yellow-rumped ("Myrtle") Warbler the throat and malar are white, creating a broad white area that contrasts abruptly with the dark auriculars. On the Nashville Warbler and Blue-headed Vireo the yellow and white throats (respectively) are more restricted, and the malar is colored gray like the auriculars. The result is that these species have a more "hooded" look with a narrower pale area only on the throat, and the reason is not just an arbitrary spreading of gray, but the coloration of an entire feather group.

Changes in Appearance with Posture

Because feathers are so flexible and can be moved around to accommodate different body positions, you can expect to see certain changes in overall color patterns as the feathers are rearranged.

Of all parts of a bird, the neck feathers, including the nape and breast feather groups, are the most changeable and variable as the posture of the bird changes. Underneath the feathers the bird's normal posture is with the neck "coiled," or retracted, and the neck feathers tightly closed together. At times the neck can be coiled even more tightly, to give the bird a more hunched and fluffed posture. At other times, the neck can be

Song Sparrow, with feathers sleeked down and neck extended (left) and feathers fluffed and neck retracted (right). Compare the feather positions and the resulting patterns in each pose.

Sparrow, showing neck extended (left) and retracted (right). Note how the changing angle of the neck feathers changes the bird's outer appearance.

uncoiled, extended, or straightened, and in this position the nape and breast feathers must spread out to cover the greater extent of the neck.

As shown by the Song Sparrow illustrations here, the fluffed feathers and coiled neck create a different pattern from the sleeked feathers and extended neck. With the neck coiled and feathers fluffed, the nape and breast feathers are compressed into a narrow ring around the neck. Streaks radiate from the center of the back and curve up from the flanks in contrast to the straighter longitudinal streaks when feathers are sleeked. In addition, the fluffed scapulars and flank feathers conceal much of the wing, and the gray bases of the scapulars are exposed.

Studying those changes is important, but it is just as important to study what does not change. Remember that even though the feathers can move up and down and from side to side, they do not change in length or shape, and they always move with the surrounding feathers. The length, shape, and arrangement of wing and tail feathers do not change, and the feather groups do not change in their relative positions. This means that color patterns change in very limited ways.

*Changes in the shape of the dark cap of a **Forster's Tern** in alert (upper), resting (middle), and crouching (lower) postures, showing how the nape feathers stretch downward as the neck is extended.*

11. Structure of Tail and Wings

The long feathers of the tail and wings, with their coverts, are unlike the feathers on other parts of the bird. These feathers are patterned differently and move differently from the body feathers, and it is necessary to make a separate study of these feathers in order to understand the overall color patterns of the wings and tail.

Tail Structure and Mechanics

Tail mechanics are similar to wing mechanics (see page 108) but much simpler, since the tail is just a fan that can be spread (open) or folded (closed). Most species have twelve tail feathers (called the rectrices), in six pairs, and the tail is always symmetrical. When the tail is closed the feathers are all stacked on top of each other, central feathers on top and outermost feathers on the bottom. Note that in this arrangement only the upperside of the central feathers and the outer edges of other feathers are visible from above, and only the underside of the outer feathers from below.

When the tail is fanned each feather is mostly visible, but still one sees primarily the outer webs from above and the inner webs from below. Many species have white markings on the outer tail feathers that show mainly when the tail is spread.

Tail feathers and the resulting tail shape are extremely variable. In many species from diverse groups the tail has been modified for display or other functions (as in pheasants, grackles, and the Scissor-tailed Flycatcher). In other species the tail is virtually nonexistent (such as grebes). The length of the tail coverts is also variable, and this determines how much of the actual tail is visible. In some species, long uppertail coverts reach almost to the end of the tail, and observers often assume that the color of these feathers is that of the actual tail. In fact, the showy feathers of a peacock's "tail" are actually highly modified uppertail coverts.

Tail shape is determined by the relative lengths of the feathers and can be an important identification clue. Most passerines have a square or slightly rounded tail with all feathers about the

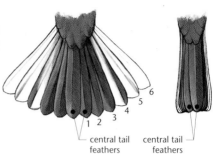

*The standard "square-tipped" tail of a **Dark-eyed Junco** from above, showing how the feathers fan out (left), exposing the mostly white outer tail feathers, then fold closed (right), concealing the outer tail feathers beneath the two central tail feathers.*

central tail feathers

central tail feathers

*Variations in tail shape: rounded, as in **Blue-gray Gnatcatcher** (left); notched, as in **Purple Finch** (center); and appearing notched, as in this **Dark-eyed Junco** (right). Note that more extreme shapes are found in other species.*

same length. In some species the central feathers are shortest and the outer feathers longer, creating a notched or forked tail, while in others the central feathers are longest and the outer feathers decidedly shorter, creating a rounded, wedge-shaped, or graduated tail.

An occasional pitfall in judging tail shape can occur when the central tail feathers shift slightly to their respective sides, displaying two separate stacks of feathers with a notch in between. Square-tailed species such as juncos can show such an apparent notch (see illustration), but closer study or a rearrangement of the feathers by the bird usually reveals the illusion.

Molt is also a factor to be considered in assessing tail shape. Growing feathers are shorter than full-grown feathers and can create various abnormal shapes depending on which feathers are missing or growing. Again, awareness and careful study should keep you from being misled.

Since tail feathers are often contrastingly colored, and because they are a part of the bird often seen (for example, as a bird disappears into dense vegetation), they can provide some useful identification clues. In many species (such as the

Blue-winged Warbler, *showing how the white pattern on the tail, as with many other species, varies with the angle of viewing and the position of the tail feathers.*

Blue-winged Warbler) the outer tail feathers are marked with patches of white. Seen from below, the tail looks mostly white at all times because these feathers dominate the view. When the tail is held closed (as it usually is) and viewed from above or from the side, no white color is visible, as only the central feathers and the outer edges of other feathers show. When the tail is spread, however, the white spots on the outer feathers become visible and create a conspicuous white flash seen from above.

It is easy to understand how a white or black band across the tip of the tail is created. Similarly, it should be apparent how minor variations in the markings on individual feathers can create subtle changes in the shape of the band. The shape and extent of white spots shown on the tails of many species can be a valuable identification clue, and understanding the difference between white corners, white sides, and a white tip on the tail is the key to identifying birds by tail pattern.

Wing Structure and Mechanics

The avian wing is a marvel of engineering—a very lightweight airfoil that folds compactly along the side of the body and doesn't interfere with walking or swimming. For the wing to fold in this way, the feathers must overlap and end up stacked on top of one another with only the outer edges showing. When the wing is spread the feathers shift and fan out to form the broad wing surface. It takes some practice to be able to recognize all the different groups of wing feathers when the wing is open as well as closed.

When folded against the body, the wing is often overlapped by the scapulars and the flank feathers, particularly during cold weather, and it may be difficult to see the wing at all. In ducks and most other swimming birds the wing is usually almost completely hidden by the body feathers. In grouse the wing may be entirely concealed—even the primaries are covered by the rump feathers.

A wing folds in two places, corresponding to the human elbow and wrist. The wrist or carpal joint is the forward point of the folded wing, usually concealed by the side feathers when the wing is folded. The names of the major wing feathers (collectively known as remiges) are determined by their point of attachment on the wing bones. The primaries are anchored to the "hand" bones; the secondaries and the tertials are anchored to the "forearm" bones.

The primaries open and close more like a fan, while the secondaries fold more like venetian blinds. When the wing is folded the primaries and secondaries end up in a stack with the tertials on top. Only the outer edge of each feather is visible; most of the primaries are hidden underneath the secondaries, and the secondary coverts are a prominent feature. Secondaries

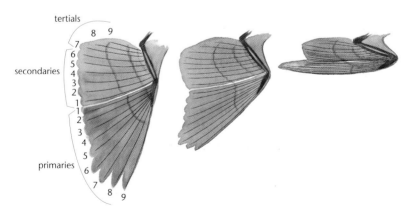

Outline of wing feathers, showing the wing bones and how they fold.

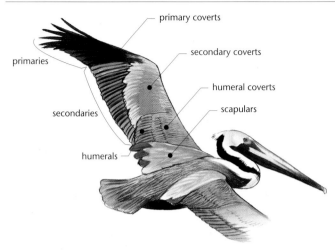

Brown Pelican, *showing structure of wing feathers on a very long-winged bird. The humerals form a more or less rectangular patch at the base of the wing.*

and primaries are numbered from the center of the wing outward (the same pattern in which most species molt).

Each feather on the wing is overlapped and protected at its base by a smaller feather. These smaller feathers, the coverts, are arranged in orderly rows across the wing. The longest wing coverts are called the greater coverts and are named for the feathers they are covering; for example, the greater secondary coverts overlap the secondaries. These are in turn overlapped by an intermediate row of coverts called the median coverts, and those are overlapped by smaller coverts known as the lesser coverts. The leading edge of the wing is covered by minute feathers called marginal coverts. In this way the whole wing is covered by a smooth streamlined surface even as it moves during flight.

The upperwing coverts are sturdier, better organized, and more distinctly patterned than the underwing coverts. On non-passerines, such as hawks, gulls, ducks, and others, the underwing coverts are nearly as extensive as the upperwing coverts and have a similar system of organization and often a bold pattern. On passerines, the underwing coverts cover only a small area and are weak and fluffy, with little or no color pattern.

On the upperside, the base of the wing is covered by the scapulars, which form two discrete patches on the sides of the back. Songbirds have relatively small and inconspicuous scapulars, and in hummingbirds the scapulars are even more reduced. In gulls and other long-winged birds the scapulars are very conspicuous and conceal most of the tertials in flight. The equivalent feathers on the underwing are the axillaries, a group of long feathers radiating from a point at the base of the wing. These are well developed in long-winged nonpasserines such as ducks, gulls, and sandpipers, but entirely absent from passerines.

In most birds the "upper arm"—the humerus bone—is short and unfeathered, but in extremely long-winged species such as pelicans there are feathers anchored to the humerus called the humerals and related humeral coverts (see illustration). These can be seen on the upperside of the spread wing in a large patch close to the body, overlapped broadly by the scapulars.

Emargination and Notch

The emargination and notch, modifications of the outer primaries, are indentations that create a narrower tip of the feather, which, when the wing is spread, give the feathers the appearance of fingers. A notch on the inner web of one feather always matches up with an emargination on the outer web of the next inner feather. The resulting "slotting" of the wingtip improves aerodynamic ability much as the flaps on planes do. Details of emargination on passerines provide some valuable clues that are useful mainly in the hand but may be visible under extraordinary field conditions. On hawks the differences are more apparent, and the number of "fingers" shown by buteos is an important clue to identifying some species.

*Outer primaries of the **Burrowing Owl**, showing the emargination and notch and how these features match up with adjacent feathers to create the narrow "fingers" of the wingtip.*

Primary Projection

The primary projection is the projection of the longest primary feathers beyond the tips of the tertials when the wing is folded. It is a useful indicator of wing structure on the folded wing and consequently an important characteristic in many groups of birds. Species with longer and more pointed wings (such as the Swainson's Thrush) generally have a longer primary projection than related species with shorter and more rounded wings (such as the Hermit Thrush), but the projection depends on the relative lengths of the primaries, tertials, and arm bones.

An objective measurement of a primary projection can be accomplished in the field by counting the number of primary tips visible beyond the longest secondaries (but be aware that angle of view can have an effect on this). A related structural clue is the length of the wingtips relative to the length of the tail, that is, whether the wingtips project beyond the tail tip or the tail beyond the wingtips, and how far.

Many open-country species such as shorebirds and pipits have very long tertials that reduce the actual primary projection. In some species such as the American Pipit the long primaries are entirely concealed beneath very long and broad

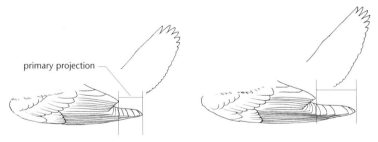

Outlines comparing pointed and rounded wingtips when the wings are open and closed: **Hermit Thrush** *(left) and* **Swainson's Thrush** *(right).*

Folded wing of **American Pipit** *(left) and* **Cedar Waxwing** *(right), demonstrating the importance of tertial length to the overall primary projection.*

tertials, resulting in no primary projection at all. On the other hand the relatively long primaries and short tertials of the Cedar Waxwing produce a long primary projection.

Wing Formula

The wing formula, useful mainly on birds in the hand, is a measurement of the relative lengths of the outer primaries, and therefore the pointedness or roundedness of the wingtip. The important points are: which primary is the longest, and details such as which inner primary is the same length as the short outermost primary. In extraordinary field conditions it may be possible to ascertain these features, and the identification of species such as *Empidonax* flycatchers might depend on such information.

Certain details can be seen in the spacing of primary tips on the folded wing and can be useful in identifying some very similar species. In general a longer and more pointed wing has more widely spaced primary tips, while a shorter and more rounded wing has very closely spaced primary tips.

Wing Patterns

The wing patterns of birds are determined by both the color and the arrangement of the feathers. The orderly arrangement of the feathers explains most of the observed patterns and is surprisingly simple once studied. The longest flight feathers—the primaries and secondaries—form the trailing portions and the tip of the wing. The rest of the wing is covered by rows of coverts arranged so that the tiniest feathers are at the leading edge of the wing, and rows of progressively larger feathers are found toward the trailing edge.

The wing coverts are often patterned, and because of the organized arrangement of the coverts, simple patterns on individual feathers create some larger plumage features. The upperwing coverts are visible only when the wing is viewed from above, and the underwing coverts only from below, so plumage features like the dark carpal bar of the Bonaparte's Gull or the wing-bars of warblers show no trace on the underside of the wing, and species such as the American Black Duck can have blackish upperwing coverts and white underwing coverts, with

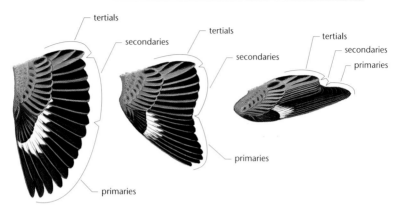

*The wing of a male **Black-throated Blue Warbler** (above) viewed from above, showing how the wing folds and how the different feather groups rearrange in each position.*

*The underwing of a male **Black-throated Blue Warbler** (right), showing how the pattern differs from below. Note that a passerine has relatively few underwing coverts.*

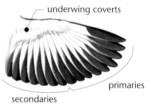

*The wing of a **Dunlin** (top), showing the major feather groups and their positions as the wing folds. Note that in this long-winged species the wing coverts are a more prominent feature of the folded wing and with the long tertials cover the flight feathers almost entirely. The pale bases of the flight feathers and white tips on the greater coverts form a wingstripe.*

*The underwing of a **Dunlin** (lower right), showing the very different pattern from below. Note the extensive and well-organized underwing coverts.*

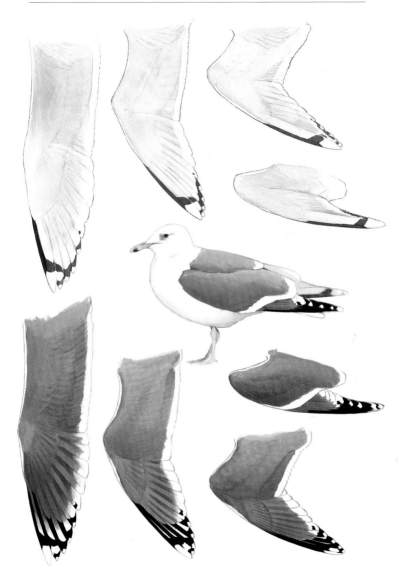

Thayer's Gull, *showing how the wing pattern changes from above and below as the wing is folded. Note how the wingtip patterns change when the primaries are fully spread, partly spread, and closed, and when seen from above and below. Notice the difference between the upperside of the folded wingtip (with tips of many primaries visible) and the underside (with only the outermost primary visible).*

*First winter **Bonaparte's Gull,** showing a common wing pattern called a carpal bar, a dark bar that runs diagonally across the coverts. Other species show many different variations on this theme. Notice also how the dark primary tips are a very significant feature on the folded wing, creating a black wingtip, but an insignificant feature on the spread wing.*

no mixing. Entirely different feathers show on the upperside and underside of the wing.

The primaries and secondaries, however, are the same feathers whether viewed from above or below. Still, they often show a very different pattern. It is common for the upperside of the primaries and secondaries to show a color unlike that on the underside of the same feathers. For example, the flight feathers of the Turkey Vulture are dark blackish brown above and silvery gray below. Furthermore, because of the overlapping of the flight feathers, patterns such as the bright blue outer edges on the secondaries of the Black-throated Blue Warbler are visible only from above, while white inner webs of the same feathers are visible only from below (see page 114).

Effects of Light on Wing Patterns

When birds are viewed from below and backlit by a bright sky, one can see the structure of the wings in the translucence of the feathers. The leading edge of the wing is dark and opaque where actual bone and muscle block the passage of light. Most of the wing is translucent, allowing some light to pass through, because the wing is nothing more than a few layers of feathers

Great Egret in flight, showing the parts of the wing that are opaque and the pattern created by the overlapping of translucent feathers.

*Wings of immature **Red-shouldered Hawk** (left row) and **Red-tailed Hawk** (right row), showing the pattern of pigmented feathers from above (top) and the resulting pattern of translucence from below (middle). Compare the actual color pattern of the underwing surface (bottom).*

tightly pressed together. All feathers must grow from the skin, so at a point just behind the wing bones light passes through not only the small coverts that are visible on the exterior at that point, but also the bases of all the larger coverts and the bases of the flight feathers. It follows that less light gets through all of these layers and the wing is nearly opaque there. Moving toward the trailing edge of the wing, beyond the tips of the small coverts and then the greater coverts, light passes only through the flight feathers themselves. The flight feathers form a regular arrangement of slightly darker stripes where adjacent feathers overlap, alternating with lighter stripes where the wing is only one feather thick. Notice how the secondaries overlap to a far greater extent than the primaries, so that the primaries allow more light to pass through.

This pattern of translucence is consistent in all species and accounts for much of the pattern seen on a backlit bird in flight. The presence of dark pigment in the feathers, however, can block some or all light from passing through. Thus, dark patterns on the flight feathers and coverts can be emphasized by backlighting, and patterns of dark and light on the upperwing can show from below in the pattern of translucence, even though the actual markings on the underwing are very different.

12. Bare Parts

The bare parts of a bird include the eye, the bill, and the legs— any part not covered by feathers. In some species there is additional bare skin around the eye or the base of the bill. The colors and patterns of these parts are often useful for identification, but they of course do not follow the same rules of appearance as feathers.

Since the skin is a living part of the bird, its color is controlled by the bird's hormones or behavioral state and can change from week to week or even moment to moment. While feathers change predictably, gradually, and irrevocably, through either wear or molt, the color of bare parts can change erratically and quickly. The facial skin of the Crested Caracara can change from bluish to reddish and back in seconds. Many species of herons and egrets undergo a transformation to intense courtship colors of facial skin and legs that last only a week or two. Virtually every species undergoes some change of bill, leg, and eye color with age or season or both; for one example, the American Goldfinch bill color changes seasonally (see page 140).

The changes in colors of bare parts do not necessarily correspond to changes in plumage color. It is common to find a bird in a nearly adultlike plumage still retaining some immature bare parts colors; or conversely, a bird with adultlike bare parts but still immature plumage.

Eye Details

Eye color is often useful in identification but must be viewed with some caution. The color of the iris can be very difficult to judge at any distance, and it is quite variable. Species that have a light-colored iris as adults generally have a dark one as immatures, and delayed maturation or other problems can cause a bird to retain a dark iris as an adult. It is not unusual to see such birds with one pale eye and one dark eye. Iris color should never be considered a very strong clue.

• **Orbital ring:** The rim of unfeathered skin immediately around the eye, usually dark but contrastingly colored in a few species.

In some species (such as certain parrots and mynas) a broad area of bare skin around the eye is called the ***periorbital.*** It is important to note that all birds have a bare orbital ring, usually dark gray; we notice it only when it is contrastingly colored (as on many gulls).

- **Iris:** The colored outer part of the eye surrounding the pupil.
- **Pupil:** The center of the eye, black in all species.

Bill Structure

Since the bill is a solid structure, not subject to the variations inherent in feathers and overall shape, details of bill shape are often a key point in identification. The bill is also the starting point for distinguishing many of the feather groups on the head, so it is important to become familiar with the basics of its structure. The relative shape and proportion of these parts can be important in separating some of our most difficult-to-identify species (such as jaegers, scaup, gulls).

- **Lower mandible:** The lower half of the bill (sometimes called simply the mandible). The point of feathers that extends onto the sides of the base of the lower mandible is called the ***malar apex.*** The feather group beginning there and running back along the sides of the lower jaw is the ***malar group.*** The point of feathers that extends onto the underside of the base of the lower mandible is called the ***ventral apex,*** and the feather group beginning there and spanning the underside of the lower jaw is the ***throat.***
- **Upper mandible:** The upper half of the bill (sometimes called the maxilla). The point of feathers that extends onto the base of the upper mandible is called the ***frontal apex.***
- **Culmen:** The upper edge of the bill as seen in profile. Subtle differences in curvature distinguish some very similar species.
- **Nail:** The tip of the upper mandible, distinctly set off from the rest of the bill on some species (but not on gulls). The exact shape and proportions of the nail can be a useful field mark.
- **Cere:** A fleshy area at the base of the upper mandible, surrounding the nostril and obvious on hawks and falcons.

nail

Mallard *showing nail at tip of bill.*

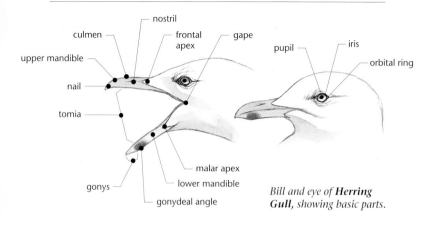

nostril
culmen
frontal apex
gape
pupil
iris
upper mandible
orbital ring
nail
tomia
malar apex
gonys
lower mandible
gonydeal angle

*Bill and eye of **Herring Gull**, showing basic parts.*

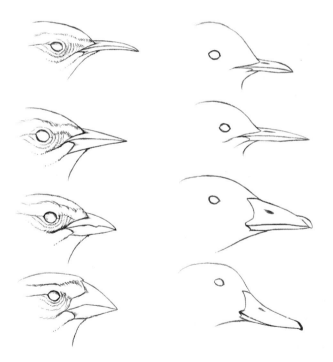

Variation in bill shapes. All species share a fundamentally similar bill structure: the gape, gonys, feathering around the base of the bill, and the bill itself have more in common among different species than not.

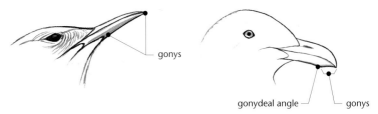

*Carolina Wren (left) showing the underside of the bill and **Herring Gull** (right) showing gonydeal angle that is conspicuous on some species at the point where the sides of the lower mandible fuse.*

- **Gonys:** The underside of the lower mandible beyond the point where the two sides of the lower mandible meet. At its base the lower mandible is relatively broad, and a groove on the underside clearly separates the sides, or ***rami*** (singular *ramus*). As the bill tapers toward the tip, the two sides of the lower mandible come closer together, eventually fusing. From that point to the tip of the bill the underside is flat or rounded. Viewed from the side, the ***gonydeal angle*** is apparent at the point where the sides of the lower mandible fuse. All species have a gonydeal angle, but it may be very inconspicuous (nearly flat) or very close to the base of the bill (as it is on most passerines).
- **Tomia** (singular *tomium*): The sharp edges of the upper and lower mandibles. Also called the cutting edges, but actually used for grasping prey.
- **Gape:** The "corners of the mouth"; the point where upper and lower mandible meet. The line extending back from this point divides the auriculars above from the malar feather group below. Also called commissure or rictus.

13. Molt

In all things of nature there is something of the marvelous.

—Aristotle

The Basics of Molt

Molt is the process by which birds replace their feathers, dropping the old ones and growing new ones. This is necessary mainly because feathers wear out over time, losing their insulating or waterproofing qualities and becoming less efficient for flight. In a few species feathers are replaced simply to provide a seasonally appropriate plumage color. All birds molt and, as a general rule, they replace all their feathers at least once a year. Molt occurs only at certain times of year, not continuously, and the timing of the process can be a useful field mark.

Other than timing, molt provides few direct clues for the identification of a species, but a knowledge of molt patterns and processes is the key to understanding plumage changes. The ability to recognize old and new feathers, and to understand feather wear, seasonal changes, and age variation, depends on an understanding of molt patterns. Molt is integral to any study of plumage variation, and a knowledge of molt patterns allows much of that variation to be categorized by age and by season. Rather than making generalizations about a species, a person familiar with molt can describe the appearance of each age and seasonal category, leading to greater precision and, ultimately, quicker and more accurate identifications.

The growth of a single primary feather of a **Yellow-billed Cuckoo.**

Each individual feather grows from a fixed point on the skin and reaches its full size in a relatively short period of time, generally a few weeks. Like human hair, once fully grown the feather

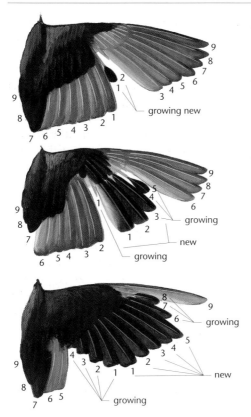

*Right wing of a one-year-old male **Scarlet Tanager,** showing normal progression of flight feather molt. The left wing should molt in a very similar and simultaneous pattern.*

is affected only by external forces such as sunlight and abrasion. The only time its color can be influenced by the hormones or diet of the bird is during the short time that the feather is growing.

Each new feather forms inside a short, horny sheath, which grows from a feather follicle in the skin. The tip of the feather is formed first and emerges from the sheath, followed incrementally by the rest of the feather. After the feather is fully grown, which may take several weeks (up to ten weeks for a large one) the sheath flakes away. Stress on the bird during feather growth, such as lack of food, can cause the growth to slow down. This may leave weak bands, called fault bars, across the grown feathers.

Molt is generally symmetrical and progresses in a predictable way. Not only does each species and each age-class usually molt at about the same time each year, each individual also molts the same feathers in about the same sequence. The molt of the large wing feathers is the most conspicuous and also the most predictable process. In songbirds such as the Scarlet Tanager (illustrated) it typically begins with the innermost primary. After several primaries have fallen, the secondaries begin to molt in sequence toward the body so that the molt progresses in two directions simultaneously from the center of the wing, although the tertials normally drop before most of the secondaries. Each primary covert molts with its respective primary, while the secondary coverts molt in advance of their respective secondaries.

Molt is a very demanding activity. A bird must grow an entirely new set of feathers (accounting for 10 to 15 percent of its body weight and requiring large amounts of protein) as quickly as possible. At the same time it must cope with increased nutritional demands to fuel the molt as well as the impairment caused by missing and growing feathers. As a general rule no species molts while engaged in other physically demanding activities such as nesting or migrating.

Each species (or population) has evolved a schedule that allows it to molt successfully at a time when food is readily available and other demands are not too high. This schedule is fairly rigid for each species but often differs between closely related species. In general, long-distance migrants (such as the Common Tern, Cliff Swallow, and Common Nighthawk) molt after fall migration on their wintering grounds in South America, while short-distance migrants (the Forster's Tern, Cave Swallow, and Lesser Nighthawk) molt before migration while still on their breeding grounds in North America. The timing of flight feather molt in these cases can be a very useful identification clue. For example, any buffy-rumped swallow molting flight feathers in the United States is likely to be a Cave Swallow, as Cliff Swallows molt in South America after fall migration.

Molt Terminology

There are primarily two different systems in use to describe the plumages and molt patterns of birds, and while they are sometimes (incorrectly) used interchangeably, they are rooted in very different concepts. The terminology most widely used by birders is the *Life Year system.* It is best to consider this terminology as describing only the appearance of the birds, and not necessarily implying the occurrence of molt, the age of the feathers, or the birds' sexual maturity. At any time during the first year of life from hatching until the following summer when it is about twelve months old, a bird is called a *first year.* The first year can be subdivided into juvenile, first winter, and first summer. In its first flying stage, just after the downy plumage worn in the nest, the bird is called a *juvenile.* Subsequent changes in appearance during the first year are labeled *first winter,* usually from about September to March, or *first summer,* usually from about April to August. At one year old most species undergo the annual complete molt to acquire the *second year* appearance (in many species this is adultlike), which is worn until the following summer. During the second year the bird may be called *second winter* or *second summer,* and so on. Once the bird reaches an adultlike appearance it is called an *adult,* whether this is in the first year, second year, or later.

The terminology that actually describes molt patterns and the resulting plumages is known as the *Humphrey-Parkes system* (H-P), named after its originators, Phillip S. Humphrey and Kenneth C. Parkes. This system is integral to any real understanding of molt in birds, leading to an understanding of age and plumage variation. I have adopted some modifications to the H-P system recently proposed by Steve N. G. Howell et al. (unpublished manuscript).

A complete molt is a molt in which all of the feathers—body, wings, and tail—are replaced. All species undergo one complete molt each year, most often in the late summer or early fall, and this molt is known as the *prebasic molt* with the resulting plumage called the *basic plumage.* All species have a basic plumage, which is renewed each year.

Many species undergo an additional partial molt each year, involving just some head and body feathers. This most often occurs in the late winter or early spring and is called the *prealternate molt,* resulting in the *alternate plumage.* Many species, but not all, have an alternate plumage. Because this is only a partial molt (not involving all feathers), the new feathers of the alternate plumage are worn alongside the older feathers of the basic plumage. The flight feathers of the wings and tail are molted only once a year, during the prebasic molt.

The H-P system indicates the age of the bird in essentially the same way as the Life-Year system. The bird is considered to be in its first year (with plumages labeled first basic and first alternate) from hatching until the prebasic molt a year later, in its second year from that time until the following prebasic molt, and so on. Whenever the appearance of the plumage reaches an adultlike stage, so that it is indistinguishable from all subsequent plumages, the bird is said to have reached the *definitive* stage. Many species acquire adultlike plumage long before they are sexually mature, and the term *definitive* refers to a mature plumage stage without implying that the bird is "adult" in any other sense.

In their first year of life most birds have a slightly different molt schedule compared to later years. The H-P system labels the plumage in the bird's first flying stage as the *juvenal plumage.* Howell et al. consider this synonymous with the first basic plumage, since it is acquired in a complete molt and will be replaced about one year later by a complete prebasic molt. Many species undergo a once-in-a-lifetime partial molt several weeks or months after leaving the nest in which they replace some of the juvenal plumage. This has traditionally been called the first prebasic molt simply because it usually results in a plumage that appears similar to that of later basic plumages. Howell et al., however, propose calling this the *preformative molt* resulting in the *formative plumage.* This small modification of the H-P system simplifies the naming of plumages in the bird's second year and later, and aligns the juvenal (first basic) plumage with subsequent basic plumages.

There are few exceptions to the general cycle outlined above. Two North American species—the Franklin's Gull and the Bobolink—have been documented to have two complete molts each year, a complete prebasic and a complete prealternate molt. A few other species have nearly complete prealternate molts, replacing some, but not all, flight feathers (for example, some sparrows and terns); or a complete preformative molt (for example, the European Starling). In a very few species an additional partial molt has been documented, and this third annual molt, whenever it occurs, is called the *presupplemental molt* resulting in the ***supplemental plumage.*** Examples include the ptarmigan and the first-year Indigo Bunting.

A practical example of the value of understanding molt patterns is knowing that the tail and wing patterns of a bird are the same for a full year, regardless of the appearance of the rest of the bird. A Magnolia Warbler's tail pattern looks the same whether it is in juvenal (first basic), formative, or first alternate plumage, because it actually retains the same tail feathers through these partial molts.

When the terms *basic, alternate, definitive,* and others were coined they were chosen because they do not link the molts and plumages to any other cycle (such as breeding/nonbreeding, summer/winter). Instead the names of plumages are linked simply to the activity of feather replacement. There are many advantages to this separation of molt terminology from other cycles. It simplifies the naming of molts and plumages and provides a terminology that can be applied to any species in any circumstances. Most important, the terms actually tell something of the underlying molt basis for the plumage and thus aid our understanding of how different species compare in their molt strategies.

There are undeniable relationships between molt and cycles of breeding and the seasons, but those relationships are not consistent across all birds, and observers should resist the inclination to simply interchange the Humphrey-Parkes and Life Year terms. The H-P system describes molt, while the Life Year system describes the birds' appearance. There is value in both systems, and field observers (who deal with appearances) should continue using the Life Year terms for most purposes. The H-P terms should be invoked only when molt is specifically addressed.

It is accurate in many cases to refer to the colorful alternate plumage acquired for part of the year as "breeding" plumage (as seen in ducks, wood-warblers, and other birds), since the function of the bright plumage seems to be courtship. Birders should feel free to continue using the term *breeding plumage* to describe such individuals, but they should keep in mind that many male ducks, for example, molt into alternate "breeding" or "summer" plumage in the fall and basic "nonbreeding" or "winter" plumage in summer. Female ducks have a substantially different molt schedule. Ptarmigan undergo striking seasonal changes not directly related to breeding; the function of their summer "breeding" plumage is concealment and not courtship. In addition, many species (including Marsh and Sedge Wrens, many sparrows, and others) go through the same prealternate ("prebreeding") molt as ducks and ptarmigan and acquire feathers indistinguishable from their basic plumage, presumably because their feathers are subject to excessive wear and must be replaced more often.

The Molt Cycle

Although the variation in molt patterns among birds may seem bewildering at first, there are really only four basic patterns of feather replacement. These four patterns include two for birds that have alternate plumages as adults and two for those that don't. The simplest strategy is known as the primitive basic strategy, then the modified basic strategy, the simple alternate strategy, and the complex alsternate strategy. The main distinc-

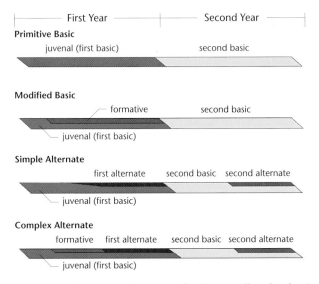

The four basic molt patterns of birds (as defined by Howell et al.), showing how the sequence of molts and plumages during the first two years of life differs in each of these strategies.

tions focus on molt in the first year of life, when young birds "catch up" to the stereotyped adult cycle of molting that is repeated every year thereafter. All passerines use the modified basic or complex alternate strategies, while nonpasserines use all four.

Humphrey-Parkes Terms

juvenal
(first basic)

definitive
basic

Life Year Terms

juvenile

adult

Sharp-shinned Hawk, *showing primitive basic molt strategy. There is a single complete molt each year. The young hawk leaves the nest with the juvenal (first basic) plumage. These are the feathers it will wear for the entire first year of life. Around the time of its first birthday it begins molting to definitive basic plumage (H-P), which the field observer would call adult. Each year thereafter the bird replaces all of its feathers in a single prebasic molt.*

Humphrey-Parkes Terms   **Life Year Terms**

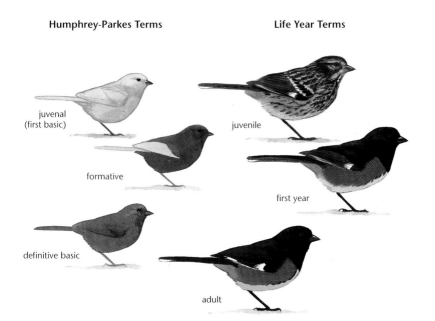

juvenal
(first basic)

juvenile

formative

first year

definitive basic

adult

Eastern Towhee, *showing modified basic molt strategy. There is a single complete molt each year, and one additional partial molt added into the first cycle. The young bird leaves the nest wearing juvenal (first basic) plumage, but this is soon mostly replaced by the formative plumage, which is worn through the first winter. Most of the large wing feathers, however, are juvenal plumage retained for the entire first year. At around one year of age the bird undergoes a complete molt and acquires the definitive basic plumage, which is typical of an adult, and this plumage is worn for a full year and replaced annually by a prebasic molt in August.*

Humphrey-Parkes Terms   **Life-Year Terms**

Herring Gull, showing simple alternate molt strategy. There is one complete and one partial molt each year, with no additional molt added into the first cycle. Adults have an alternate plumage and first year birds have a modified version of this molt. The young bird leaves the nest wearing juvenal plumage, and over the first winter an individual undergoes a variable molt that involves from a few to many head and body feathers (traditionally this was thought to be two molts). In its first summer, when about one year old, the Herring Gull then has a complete prebasic molt into second basic plumage. After this it follows the adult pattern of a complete prebasic molt from late summer into winter and a partial prealternate molt in late winter and spring.

Humphrey-Parkes Terms   **Life Year Terms**

juvenal
(first basic)

formative

first alternate

juvenile

first winter

first summer

definitive
basic

definitive
alternate

adult winter/
nonbreeding

adult summer/
breeding

Scarlet Tanager, showing complex alternate molt strategy. There is one complete and one partial molt each year, and an additional partial molt added into the first cycle. The tanager leaves the nest wearing the juvenal (first basic) plumage. Soon after fledging, a partial molt results in the formative plumage, which is worn through the first winter. This is followed in the spring by another partial molt to first alternate plumage, which is worn through the first summer. At the end of the first summer, at about one year of age, the bird undergoes a complete molt (finally replacing the juvenal wing feathers) and acquires the definitive basic plumage, the adult nonbreeding appearance worn through the winter. In late winter the bird undergoes a partial molt to the definitive alternate plumage, the adult breeding appearance, which will be worn through the summer. This cycle then repeats in all subsequent years, a complete molt in late summer and a partial molt in late winter.

Molt and Feather Wear

It is important to recognize that not all changes in feather appearance are the result of molt, and molt alone does not explain all variations. Individual birds have a certain appearance because of a combination of molt (in all its permutations), the extent of feather wear and fading, and the colors of the bare parts. Consider birds like the Snow Bunting and the House Sparrow, which acquire a breeding appearance through wear of their feathers. The H-P terminology would label the plumage all year simply as *definitive basic,* because no molt has occurred, regardless of the bird's appearance. This is unsatisfactory for the field observer, because the May bird looks so different from the September bird. The Life Year system labels the fall bird as *adult*

Humphrey-Parkes Terms

juvenal
(first basic)

formative

definitive basic

Life Year Terms

juvenile

first winter

first summer

adult
nonbreeding

adult breeding

Snow Bunting, *showing phases of modified basic molt strategy with different appearance acquired by wear. The molt cycle of this species is identical to that of the Eastern Towhee. The bunting leaves the nest wearing juvenal (first basic) plumage but molts quickly to formative plumage, retaining the juvenal flight feathers. No other molt occurs until the definitive prebasic molt the following year, and only one molt each year thereafter. Feather wear alone produces the striking first breeding and adult breeding appearance, as pale brownish feather tips wear away.*

nonbreeding (*adult winter*) and the spring bird as *adult breeding* (*adult summer*). This acknowledges the striking and predictable difference in appearance but does not inform us about the underlying process and the fact that the transition occurs gradually over a period of months.

The Effects of Molt on Appearance

The process of molt and the loss and growth of feathers has some direct effects on appearance. The most frequent is the mixture of old and new, fresh and worn, breeding and non-breeding feathers during the changeover to a new plumage. At the same time, the different lengths of growing feathers can give the bird an unkempt, "messy" appearance. Missing and growing feathers create gaps in the wings or tail, and can result in abnormal tail shapes or sometimes a missing tail, but learning to recognize gaps that are caused by molt can take some practice. Other, more subtle effects of molt can include the loss or reduction of small markings, the appearance of odd white or gray patches as feather bases are exposed, and even changes in flight style as wing shape is altered.

The Western Sandpiper illustrated below might take a few weeks to molt from the very dark and worn alternate plumage to the fresh pale gray feathers of basic plumage. During this period the bird has a "messy" salt-and-pepper pattern that is a characteristic sign of molt. Semipalmated Sandpipers undergo a similar stage, but weeks later than the average Western Sandpiper. Least Sandpipers molt as well, but because the incoming basic feathers are rather dark brownish they do not contrast so

Western Sandpiper, near the end of the prebasic molt, molting to basic plumage and changing from worn breeding appearance to nonbreeding appearance.

obviously with the worn alternate feathers, and the bird never acquires this salt-and-pepper plumage aspect.

The Ring-billed Gull illustrated below shows the progress of molt through the wings. With the inner primaries missing there is an obvious gap; the wingbeats might be quicker and "sloppier," as the outer primaries move a little more independently from the rest of the wing.

For a brief period when molt reaches the outer primaries, the longest outer primaries are missing, and the next-to-outer primaries are growing. The effect is to create atypically short and rounded wingtips with very limited black color. Wingbeats will be relatively quick and choppy. With greatly reduced black in the wingtips and an unusual flight style, a molting Ring-billed Gull can easily be mistaken in a brief or distant view for a rarer

Ring-billed Gull, *showing the progression of molt through the primaries. Soon after molt begins (upper left) the molt gap is in the inner primaries. Later (upper right), molt has reached the outer primaries, and the outermost feathers are missing or growing. Finally (lower) molt is complete, and all feathers have grown in.*

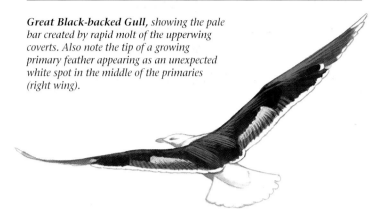

Great Black-backed Gull, *showing the pale bar created by rapid molt of the upperwing coverts. Also note the tip of a growing primary feather appearing as an unexpected white spot in the middle of the primaries (right wing).*

species such as the Iceland Gull, but this stage should occur only during the months of August and September and should not cause the observer more than momentary confusion. Among other species that require careful study of flight style, wing shape, or wingtip pattern, such as storm-petrels and hawks, similar molt stages can make identification much more challenging.

In most cases molt proceeds slowly and on scattered feathers so that the feather coat remains essentially unbroken. Sometimes, however, molt can create gaps in the coat that reveal the gray or whitish color of the feather bases below. These gaps are perhaps most frequently seen on the upperwing coverts of long-winged species such as gulls, terns, ravens, and shearwaters. Rapid molt of the secondary coverts results in large blocks of feathers dropping almost simultaneously, exposing the bases of the flight feathers or other coverts. The effect is barely noticeable on a pale gray species such as the Ring-billed Gull; there is simply a slight patchiness where the paler feather bases show. On dark-backed species such as the Great Black-backed Gull, however, the effect can be striking, as a whitish bar appears across an otherwise blackish surface.

Hormonal Control of Feather Pigment
Seasonal changes in feather color are controlled by varying levels of hormones during feather growth. While most birds molt

a "pure" coat of breeding or nonbreeding, male or female, adult or immature feathers, it is not unusual to find individual feathers with intermediate colors or patterns. Birds develop feathers with wide variations in the brightness and extent of colors, depending on the levels of hormones at the time of feather growth. This variation can be seen in spring and summer shorebirds; even within a single molt, feathers can develop that range from plain nonbreeding colors to bright breeding colors. This can result in an appearance in between breeding and nonbreeding, such as drab or poorly marked breeding plumage or bright nonbreeding plumage.

*Scapulars of a **Red Knot** in basic plumage, showing individual feathers with an intermediate pattern. All of these feathers are fresh, pale gray with neat pale tips and no obvious wear, but some of them have small black and rusty markings centrally, suggesting breeding plumage. At the time these feathers were growing, the bird had enough breeding hormones in its bloodstream to partially "activate" the feather follicle to deposit some breeding color in the growing feather.*

14. Feather Wear

Feathers are continually subjected to the degrading effects of the environment from the moment they grow. The two primary effects are wear and fading. The resulting gradual change in shape and color of feathers can lead to dramatic changes in appearance over time. Many species (such as the Snow Bunting shown and described on page 134) take advantage of this and simply allow their bright courtship/breeding plumage to develop as feather tips wear away, revealing the colors that were deposited in the previous autumn. In this way they can acquire a showy plumage without having to invest in the energy- and time-consuming process of growing new feathers.

Feathers wear by rubbing against plants and soil as well as against the bird's own beak during preening. Wear physically removes material from the edges of the feather and changes its appearance by making the feather look ragged and uneven. In many cases wear also removes a contrastingly colored edge and shortens the feather to expose another color on the feather below. Pale feathers or parts of feathers are much more susceptible to wear than dark feathers, as the melanin pigment responsible for dark colors actually strengthens the feather.

Feathers fade mainly through bleaching by the sun. Sunlight breaks down pigments and renders the feathers paler and less colorful. Certain pigments are more susceptible to fading than others, such as the pale reddish-brown colors that are common in shorebirds and in juvenile hawks and terns. Other colors, such as black, are more resistant to fading.

Feather wear and fading work in tandem with molt to produce the range of appearances we see in the field. In fact, contrasts between old and new feathers (known as molt limits) are often the only visible evidence of molt. When we talk about a field observer's study of molt, we are often talking about a study of feather wear. Molt is inferred by the presence of molt limits, and molt schedules provide the framework to understand the variation in feather wear.

The appearance of the American Goldfinch at various times of year is strikingly different. Careful examination shows that this is due to a combination of molt and the effects of wear and

American Goldfinch, *showing fresh and worn plumages. Upper two birds in basic plumage, the typical winter/nonbreeding appearance: when fresh, around October (left), and worn, around January (right). Lower two birds in alternate plumage, the summer/breeding appearance: when fresh, around March (left), and worn, around August (right).*

fading. Beginning in fall we see a bird in fresh basic plumage (all feathers new), richly colored brown and gray, with cinnamon wing markings and the yellow of the throat and face mostly obscured. As the feathers wear and fade, the yellow throat is exposed (helped along by the molt of a few feathers there), and the wingbars wear and become slightly thinner and fade to mostly white.

Molt of the body feathers to alternate plumage in February and March produces a relatively sudden change to brilliant yellow body plumage and a black forehead, but the wing and tail feathers are still retained basic plumage from the previous fall, and the pale markings along the edges of the wing feathers have become still thinner and all white. By late summer, after nearly twelve months, the pale tips of the coverts that formed the wingbars, along with the pale edges of the secondaries and

Western Sandpiper in fresh (left) and worn (right) alternate plumage, with representative scapular feathers from each, showing the striking changes that take place gradually, over a period of about four months, with no molt. Most field guides can show only one example of each plumage, so they illustrate an "average" bird, somewhere between these extremes.

primaries, are almost completely lost, and the yellow feathers show uneven color and bits of white where they are worn.

Some species become darker overall with wear and fading, and others become paler. In the case of the Western Sandpiper, illustrated above, the weak whitish feather tips wear off, exposing the wear- and fade-resistant blackish markings underneath. The reddish colors fade and wear as well, and the worn bird is dominated by the blackish feather centers.

On the Ring-billed Gull (illustrated below), the first winter feather markings are all brown, so the combined effects of sub-

*First year **Ring-billed Gull**, showing fresh appearance, as in October (left), and worn appearance, as in June (right), with representative wing coverts from each.*

stantial wear and fading create a much paler and essentially unmarked bird. Even the shape of the bird is noticeably affected, as the worn individual is thinner and shaggier, less full and sleek, than the fresh one.

Juvenal feathers of many species, like this Ring-billed Gull, are particularly weak and subject to bleaching and wear. They wear faster and fade more than adult feathers under the same conditions. The most faded and worn gulls are first summer birds still retaining juvenal feathers. A bird in this condition is overdue for molting. Most birds that look so worn will also show a few new feathers as the molt to the next plumage begins.

Red-tailed Hawks *soaring,*
adult female on left and juvenile
male on right, showing age-
related differences in shape and
color, along with sex-related
differences in size. These
differences could easily lead an
observer to think that these are
two different species.

15. Age Variation

In many species, the difference between adult and immature is of no importance in the identification process. However, in very similar and confusing species such as sandpipers, hawks, gulls, and flycatchers, it may be critical to know the age or sex of the bird before you reach an identification.

Determination of the age of a bird depends to some extent on details of plumage patterns but more on broad patterns of molt and feather characteristics. There are general rules that apply to age variation of all hawks; similar rules apply to all shorebirds, all warblers, and other groups as well. To familiarize yourself with age variations, carefully watch a few nearby individuals before you try to pick out details and feather patterns on more distant birds.

The molt strategies outlined in the chapter "Molt" provide clues for some basic methods of "aging" (determining the age of) birds. One clue, which applies to virtually all species and can be very useful in late summer and fall, is that juveniles, having just fledged, are then in very uniform fresh plumage, while adults are actively molting or showing a mixture of old and new plumage. Juvenal plumage of loons, shorebirds, hawks, gulls, geese, ducks, and most other nonpasserines is characterized by relatively small pointed feathers that are all neatly lined up and often edged with crisp white, gold, or rufous colors. Once you learn this extremely neat appearance, it alone is often enough to enable you to age a bird in the fall. As juvenal plumage wears the differences become less obvious, but details of feather shape and pattern can still allow aging into the first winter, and in many species throughout the first year.

Hawks undergo just a single molt each year; therefore, they wear their juvenal (first basic) plumage for a full year before it is replaced by the second basic plumage. The juvenal flight feathers of a hawk are relatively longer, more pointed, narrower, and paler than those of the adult. The wings and tail look neat throughout the first year, with all feathers about the same length, all pointed, all with a matching color pattern. During the prebasic molt at age one year, the hawk replaces some but not all of the juvenal flight feathers (this incomplete replacement is common in large birds, which might take three years to complete the wing molt cycle). With molt limits where the new second basic feathers are mixed among retained juvenal feathers, the wings of the one-year-old hawk have a patchy look. The second basic feathers are adultlike—shorter, blunter, and darker

Western Sandpiper, showing the difference in feather arrangement between fresh juvenal plumage (left) and the adult plumage (right).

*Three age classes of **Swainson's Hawk**—juvenile/first year (left), second year (middle), and adult (right)—showing different molt stages and how molt limits, feather shape and pattern, and differential feather wear can be used for determining a bird's age.*

than the juvenal feathers—and they stand out in pattern and in shape. By the age of two, another prebasic molt replaces the remaining juvenal feathers, so that the wing is now relatively uniform in feather shape and pattern; but it still shows molt limits, or contrasts between feathers from the previous year's molt and new feathers.

You can see how the progress of molt leaves clues that allow a birder to determine the age of a hawk. A complete set of juvenal feathers indicates a bird in its first year of life. A mixture of adultlike feathers with molt limits and some retained juvenal flight feathers indicates a bird in its second year, and a full set of adultlike feathers indicates a bird in its third year or later.

In passerines the juvenal plumage is loose, weakly marked, and soon molted for a plumage similar to that of the adult. Yet that molt provides another clue for aging these birds. Most passerines have only a partial preformative molt in their first fall, replacing most of the juvenal plumage but retaining the large juvenal wing and tail feathers. The resulting contrast between new coverts (and often tertials), with old juvenal secondaries and primaries, is sometimes apparent in the field and

Scarlet Tanager first year male, showing contrast between new black tertials and coverts and old brownish secondaries and primaries.

can be used to age these birds until their prebasic molt a year later.

The differences are most obvious on birds that acquire new black feathers, for example the Scarlet Tanager or Eastern Towhee, and the contrast between black coverts and brownish secondaries is a sure sign of a bird less than a year old. In species with all brown or olive wing feathers, the difference between old and new feathers is much less obvious, but it can still sometimes be seen with experience and close study.

The primaries of terns provide an excellent clue to the bird's age, as shown on the adult and juvenile Sandwich Tern below. A number of minor differences can be seen to distinguish these two age classes—the juvenile lacks the yellow bill tip and has

Sandwich Tern juvenile (left), showing uniform primaries, and adult (right), showing molt limit, around October.

dark marks on the tertials, a darker carpal bar, and subtly pale-mottled wing coverts—but the most obvious difference is in the primaries. The juvenile has all new primaries, all a uniform dark gray color, which will become darker with wear. The adult has a mixture: old worn outer primaries that are very dark and a few new inner primaries that are very pale gray. This obvious evidence of molt—new and old feathers together—is enough to distinguish the older bird from the juvenile.

16. Ethics and Conservation

To a person uninstructed in natural history, his country- or sea-side stroll is a walk through a gallery filled with wonderful works of art, nine-tenths of which have their faces turned to the wall.
—Thomas Huxley

An unfortunate consequence of the great increase in the popularity of birding is the impact it has on the birds. The principal ethical rule for bird-watchers should be to have no such impact. Even in the very places that have been set aside as sanctuaries, constant pressure from bird-watchers can have a detrimental effect on the birds. If you are approaching birds, and they adopt an upright alarmed posture, it is time to stop and allow them to settle back down. Also remember that in crowded areas, such as a beach, many birds are subject to disturbance throughout the day. And be especially conscious of your actions around nesting and roosting birds, which are more sensitive to disturbance then than at other times.

Willets *in relaxed posture, resting (above), and in alert posture when alarmed or nervous (below).*

"Pishing" (see the chapter "Finding Birds") is a form of harassment, as is using tape recordings of calls to attract birds. The effect of these small disturbances may be negligible when they are isolated events, but when they are repeated hour after hour and day after day, especially around nesting or roosting birds, they can have a negative impact by distracting the birds from the necessities of survival, such as feeding, avoiding predators, and resting.

Conservation

Bird populations of many species are declining and face multiple threats, including habitat loss, pesticides, and predation by house cats. As birders we are in a unique position to see and document these problems—and to help find solutions. Live in an environmentally friendly way. Encourage other people to see the beauty and value of birds and a healthy environment. Support habitat preservation. Work locally. Your support of local, national, and international conservation organizations is also important.

The Nature Conservancy
4245 North Fairfax Drive, Suite 100
Arlington, VA 22203-1606
(800) 628-6860
www.nature.org

National Audubon Society
700 Broadway
New York, NY 10003
(212) 979-3000
www.audubon.org

American Bird Conservancy
P.O. Box 249
4249 Loudoun Avenue
The Plains, VA 20198
(540) 253-5780
www.abcbirds.org

Latin Names for Species Mentioned in the Text

The names in this list follow the standard species classification set by the American Ornithologists' Union's (AOU) *Check-list of North American Birds*.

Bittern, Least *(Ixobrychus exilis)*
Blackbird, Red-winged *(Agelaius phoeniceus)*
Bobolink *(Dolichonyx oryzivorus)*
Bunting, Indigo *(Passerina cyanea)*
Bunting, Snow *(Plectrophenax nivalis)*
Caracara, Crested *(Caracara cheriway)*
Cardinal, Northern *(Cardinalis cardinalis)*
Chat, Yellow-breasted *(Icteria virens)*
Chickadee, Black-capped *(Poecile atricapilla)*
Chickadee, Carolina *(Poecile carolinensis)*
Crane, Sandhill *(Grus canadensis)*
Cuckoo, Yellow-billed *(Coccyzus americanus)*
Dowitcher, Short-billed *(Limnodromus griseus)*
Duck, American Black *(Anas rubripes)*
Duck, Ring-necked *(Aythya collaris)*
Dunlin *(Calidris alpina)*
Egret, Great *(Ardea alba)*
Falcon, Peregrine *(Falco peregrinus)*
Finch, House *(Carpodacus mexicanus)*
Finch, Purple *(Carpodacus purpureus)*
Flicker, Northern *(Colaptes auratus)*
Flycatcher, Hammond's *(Empidonax hammondii)*
Flycatcher, Scissor-tailed *(Tyrannus forficatus)*
Flycatcher, Yellow-bellied *(Empidonax flaviventris)*
Gnatcatcher, Blue-gray *(Polioptila caerulea)*
Goldfinch, American *(Carduelis tristis)*
Goose, Canada *(Branta canadensis)*
Grosbeak, Black-headed *(Pheucticus melanocephalus)*
Grosbeak, Blue *(Guiraca caerulea)*
Grosbeak, Rose-breasted *(Pheucticus ludovicianus)*
Gull, Bonaparte's *(Larus philadelphia)*

Gull, Franklin's *(Larus pipixcan)*
Gull, Glaucous *(Larus hyperboreus)*
Gull, Glaucous-winged *(Larus glaucescens)*
Gull, Great Black-backed *(Larus marinus)*
Gull, Herring *(Larus argentatus)*
Gull, Iceland *(Larus glaucoides)*
Gull, Laughing *(Larus atricilla)*
Gull, Mew *(Larus canus)*
Gull, Ring-billed *(Larus delawarensis)*
Gull, Thayer's *(Larus thayeri)*
Gull, Western *(Larus occidentalis)*
Gyrfalcon *(Falco rusticolus)*
Harrier, Northern *(Circus cyaneus)*
Hawk, Cooper's *(Accipiter cooperii)*
Hawk, Red-shouldered *(Buteo lineatus)*
Hawk, Red-tailed *(Buteo jamaicensis)*
Hawk, Sharp-shinned *(Accipiter striatus)*
Hawk, Swainson's *(Buteo swainsoni)*
Heron, Black-crowned Night- *(Nycticorax nycticorax)*
Heron, Great Blue *(Ardea herodias)*
Hummingbird, Allen's *(Selasphorus sasin)*
Hummingbird, Black-chinned *(Archilochus alexandri)*
Hummingbird, Calliope *(Stellula calliope)*
Hummingbird, Ruby-throated *(Archilochus colubris)*
Hummingbird, Rufous *(Selasphorus rufus)*
Jay, Blue *(Cyanocitta cristata)*
Junco, Dark-eyed *(Junco hyemalis)*
Killdeer *(Charadrius vociferus)*
Knot, Red *(Calidris canutus)*
Lark, Sky *(Alauda arvensis)*
Longspur, Smith's *(Calcarius pictus)*
Loon, Common *(Gavia immer)*
Loon, Red-throated *(Gavia stellata)*
Mallard *(Anas platyrhynchos)*
Meadowlark, Eastern *(Sturnella magna)*
Meadowlark, Western *(Sturnella neglecta)*
Merganser, Common *(Mergus merganser)*
Merganser, Hooded *(Lophodytes cucullatus)*
Merganser, Red-breasted *(Mergus serrator)*
Mockingbird, Northern *(Mimus polyglottos)*

Nighthawk, Common *(Chordeiles minor)*
Nighthawk, Lesser *(Chordeiles acutipennis)*
Nuthatch, Red-breasted *(Sitta canadensis)*
Nuthatch, White-breasted *(Sitta carolinensis)*
Oriole, Audubon's *(Icterus graduacauda)*
Oriole, Baltimore *(Icterus galbula)*
Oriole, Bullock's *(Icterus bullockii)*
Owl, Burrowing *(Athene cunicularia)*
Owl, Eastern Screech- *(Otus asio)*
Pelican, Brown *(Pelecanus occidentalis)*
Pintail, Northern *(Anas acuta)*
Pipit, American *(Anthus rubescens)*
Plover, American Golden- *(Pluvialis dominica)*
Plover, Black-bellied *(Pluvialis squatarola)*
Plover, Piping *(Charadrius melodus)*
Plover, Semipalmated *(Charadrius semipalmatus)*
Quail, California *(Callipepla californica)*
Redshank, Spotted *(Tringa erythropus)*
Robin, American *(Turdus migratorius)*
Sandpiper, Least *(Calidris minutilla)*
Sandpiper, Semipalmated *(Calidris pusilla)*
Sandpiper, Spoonbill *(Eurynorhynchus pygmeus)*
Sandpiper, Spotted *(Actitis macularia)*
Sandpiper, Western *(Calidris mauri)*
Sandpiper, White-rumped *(Calidris fuscicollis)*
Sapsucker, Yellow-bellied *(Sphyrapicus varius)*
Scoter, White-winged *(Melanitta fusca)*
Siskin, Pine *(Carduelis pinus)*
Snipe, Common *(Gallinago gallinago)*
Sparrow, Fox *(Passerella iliaca)*
Sparrow, Golden-crowned *(Zonotrichia atricapilla)*
Sparrow, House *(Passer domesticus)*
Sparrow, Savannah *(Passerculus sandwichensis)*
Sparrow, Song *(Melospiza melodia)*
Sparrow, White-crowned *(Zonotrichia leucophrys)*
Sparrow, White-throated *(Zonotrichia albicollis)*
Starling, European *(Sturnus vulgaris)*
Swallow, Cave *(Petrochelidon fulva)*
Swallow, Cliff *(Petrochelidon pyrrhonota)*
Swan, Tundra *(Cygnus columbianus)*

Tanager, Scarlet *(Piranga olivacea)*
Tanager, Summer *(Piranga rubra)*
Tanager, Western *(Piranga ludoviciana)*
Teal, Blue-winged *(Anas discors)*
Tern, Common *(Sterna hirundo)*
Tern, Forster's *(Sterna forsteri)*
Tern, Roseate *(Sterna dougallii)*
Tern, Sandwich *(Sterna sandvicensis)*
Thrasher, Brown *(Toxostoma rufum)*
Thrush, Hermit *(Catharus guttatus)*
Thrush, Swainson's *(Catharus ustulatus)*
Thrush, Varied *(Ixoreus naevius)*
Titmouse, Bridled *(Baeolophus wollweberi)*
Towhee, Eastern *(Pipilo erythrophthalmus)*
Veery *(Catharus fuscescens)*
Vireo, Black-capped *(Vireo atricapillus)*
Vireo, Blue-headed *(Vireo solitarius)*
Vireo, Red-eyed *(Vireo olivaceus)*
Vireo, Warbling *(Vireo gilvus)*
Vireo, White-eyed *(Vireo griseus)*
Vulture, Turkey *(Cathartes aura)*
Warbler, Blackpoll *(Dendroica striata)*
Warbler, Black-throated Blue *(Dendroica caerulescens)*
Warbler, Black-throated Green *(Dendroica virens)*
Warbler, Blue-winged *(Vermivora pinus)*
Warbler, Chestnut-sided *(Dendroica pensylvanica)*
Warbler, Connecticut *(Oporornis agilis)*
Warbler, Golden-winged *(Vermivora chrysoptera)*
Warbler, Magnolia *(Dendroica magnolia)*
Warbler, Nashville *(Vermivora ruficapilla)*
Warbler, Orange-crowned *(Vermivora celata)*
Warbler, Palm *(Dendroica palmarum)*
Warbler, Prairie *(Dendroica discolor)*
Warbler, Tennessee *(Vermivora peregrina)*
Warbler, Townsend's *(Dendroica townsendi)*
Warbler, Yellow *(Dendroica petechia)*
Warbler, Yellow-rumped *(Dendroica coronata)*
Waterthrush, Northern *(Seiurus noveboracensis)*
Waxwing, Cedar *(Bombycilla cedrorum)*
Whip-poor-will *(Caprimulgus vociferus)*

Willet *(Catoptrophorus semipalmatus)*
Woodcock, American *(Scolopax minor)*
Woodpecker, Downy *(Picoides pubescens)*
Woodpecker, Hairy *(Picoides villosus)*
Woodpecker, Lewis's *(Melanerpes lewis)*
Woodpecker, Pileated *(Dryocopus pileatus)*
Woodpecker, Red-headed *(Melanerpes erythrocephalus)*
Wren, Carolina *(Thryothorus ludovicianus)*
Wren, House *(Troglodytes aedon)*
Wren, Marsh *(Cistothorus palustris)*
Wren, Sedge *(Cistothorus platensis)*
Wren, Winter *(Troglodytes troglodytes)*
Yellowlegs, Greater *(Tringa melanoleuca)*
Yellowlegs, Lesser *(Tringa flavipes)*
Yellowthroat, Common *(Geothlypis trichas)*

Notes

Notes

Notes

Notes